NATIONAL MISSILE DEFENSE: ISSUES AND DEVELOPMENTS

NATIONAL MISSILE DEFENSE: ISSUES AND DEVELOPMENTS

ERIN V. CAUSEWELL (EDITOR)

Novinka Books
New York

Senior Editors: Susan Boriotti and Donna Dennis
Coordinating Editor: Tatiana Shohov
Office Manager: Annette Hellinger
Graphics: Wanda Serrano
Editorial Production: Jennifer Vogt, Matthew Kozlowski, Jonathan Rose and Maya Columbus
Circulation: Ave Maria Gonzalez, Vera Popovich, Luis Aviles, Melissa Diaz, Nicolas Miro and Jeannie Pappas
Communications and Acquisitions: Serge P. Shohov
Marketing: Cathy DeGregory

Library of Congress Cataloging-in-Publication Data
Available Upon Request

ISBN: 1-59033-247-4.

Copyright © 2002 by Novinka Books, An Imprint of
Nova Science Publishers, Inc.
400 Oser Ave, Suite 1600
Hauppauge, New York 11788-3619
Tele. 631-231-7269   Fax 631-231-8175
e-mail: Novascience@earthlink.net
Web Site: http://www.novapublishers.com

All rights reserved. No part of this book may be reproduced, stored in a retrieval system or transmitted in any form or by any means: electronic, electrostatic, magnetic, tape, mechanical photocopying, recording or otherwise without permission from the publishers.

The publisher has taken reasonable care in the preparation of this book, but makes no expressed or implied warranty of any kind and assumes no responsibility for any errors or omissions. No liability is assumed for incidental or consequential damages in connection with or arising out of information contained in this book.

This publication is designed to provide accurate and authoritative information with regard to the subject matter covered herein. It is sold with the clear understanding that the publisher is not engaged in rendering legal or any other professional services. If legal or any other expert assistance is required, the services of a competent person should be sought. FROM A DECLARATION OF PARTICIPANTS JOINTLY ADOPTED BY A COMMITTEE OF THE AMERICAN BAR ASSOCIATION AND A COMMITTEE OF PUBLISHERS.

Printed in the United States of America

CONTENTS

Preface		**vii**
Chapter 1	Missile Defense: The Current Debate *Steven A. Hildreth and Amy F. Woolf*	1
Chapter 2	National Missile Defense: Issues for Congress *Steven A. Hildreth and Amy F. Woolf*	75
Chapter 3	National Missile Defense: Russia's Reaction *Amy F. Woolf*	99
Index		**129**

PREFACE

Missiles came of age after World War II and the United States has pursued missile defenses ever since. The issue has turned out to be one of the most divisive of the past generation taking into account the Russian position and their threat or perceived threat and the technical difficulties of actually implementing any missile defense. The Bush Administration claims that for the first time an effective missile defense is technically possible and that the threat of weapons of mass destruction has spread to many nations and groups other than Russia. The two factors, according to them, make missile defense a urgent priority justifying the breaking of the widely-revered ABM Treaties. Their argument rests partially on a bet that the Russians have now fallen so far behind since the Yeltsin government took over that they cannot keep up technologically. Although terrorism groups will not be deterred by the missile defense being planned, countries like China, North Korea etc might well be. This book frames the current debate and also presents the legal considerations for withdrawal from the ABM Treaties.

Chapter 1

MISSILE DEFENSE: THE CURRENT DEBATE

Steven A. Hildreth and Amy F. Woolf

SUMMARY

The United States has pursued missile defenses since the dawn of the missile age shortly after World War II. The development and deployment of missile defenses has not only been elusive, but has proven to be one of the most divisive issues of the past generation.

The Bush Administration has substantially altered the debate over missile defenses. The Administration requested significant funding increases for missile defense programs (about 61 percent above that approved by Congress for FY2001), eliminated the distinction between national and theater missile defense, restructured the missile defense program to focus more directly on developing deployment options for a "layered" capability to intercept missiles aimed at U.S. territory across the whole spectrum of their flight path, adopted a new, untried development and acquisition strategy, and announced U.S. withdrawal from the 1972 Anti-ballistic Missile Treaty.

The Administration has argues these steps were necessary in response to growing concerns over the spread of weapons of mass destruction and their means of delivery, especially on the part of a handful of potentially hostile states and terrorists. In addition, they asserted that U.S. deterrence theory has outlived its usefulness, and that it could not be relied upon to dissuade unstable leaders in rogue states.

Critics take issue with assertions that the threat is increasing, citing evidence that the number of nations seeking or possessing nuclear weapons has actually declined over the past twenty years. Moreover, they argue that the technology for effective missile defense remains immature, that deployment is provocative to allies, friends, and adversaries, and it is a budget-buster that reduces the availability of funds to modernize and operate U.S. conventional military forces. They argue especially that major powers will view U.S. missile defense as an attempt at strategic domination and that some, such as China, will expand its missile capabilities in response.

The Bush Administration's plans raise a number of issues, many of which are examined in this report. The issues that have received attention in the 107th Congress, are: 1) U.S. compliance with the ABM Treaty and now the announced withdrawal from the Treaty; 2) a new acquisition concept for developing missile defense that does not lend itself readily to oversight, system definition, or cost and effectiveness analysis; and, 3) the restructuring of existing missile defense programs within the Missile Defense Agency (formerly BMDO).

MOST RECENT DEVELOPMENTS

In early May, 2002, the House Armed Services Committee approved $7.784 billion for ballistic missile defense and related activities in its version of the FY2003 Defense Authorization Bill (H.R. 4546). This represents an increase of $21 million over the budget request of $7.763 billion. In its legislation, the Committee transferred responsibility for MEADs program and the PAC-3 program back to the Missile Defense Agency (MDA), rejecting the Administration's attempt to move these programs to the Army.

On April 15, the Missile Defense Agency announced that it had restructured the SBIRS-low program, which has been the source of much controversy. In its initial budget submission, the Pentagon had indicated that it would delay the launch of the first satellite from 2006 to 2008, but the new plan calls for the launch of two demonstration satellites in 2006 or 2007. These satellites will have less capability than those planned for the full constellation. DOD still has not settled on an eventual architecture, and therefore, cannot estimate the eventual system cost.

OVERVIEW

Issues for Congress

In July 2001, the Bush Administration presented to Congress the outlines of its proposed approach to missile defense. The Bush Administration's plan differs significantly from the approach pursued by the Clinton Administration. The issue for Congress was whether to approve, modify, or reject the Bush Administration's proposed approach for missile defense. (A section on current congressional action is found at the end of this report.) In general, Congress supported the President's FY 2002 request, making some adjustments in programs experiencing technical problems and reducing funding for programs that Congress was not yet willing to commit to for early or crisis deployment purposes.

Congress' decisions on these issues in FY 2002 and this coming year will likely have significant implications for U.S. military capabilities, arms control, defense funding requirements and the composition of U.S. defense spending, as well as U.S. relations with other countries.

Scope of Report

This report provides background information on the Bush Administration's proposed approach, and discussed key issues relating to it. Key issues raised in the next section include:

ABM Treaty Issues
What are the implications of the Administration's announcement to withdraw from the ABM Treaty? When and how will the Administration's program "bump up" against the limits in the ABM Treaty? What are the prospects for success in the discussions with Russia to move beyond the ABM Treaty and develop a new strategic framework?

Budget Issues

How will the money for missile defense be allocated among the different elements of the program? How will increased funding for missile defense affect funding for other programs in the defense budget?

Technology Issues

Will the United States be able to develop and deploy missile defenses that can intercept missiles of all ranges at all phases of their flights? If not, can a partial system be overcome even by rogue states? What are the key technological challenges? When might the research and development program give way to a deployment program? Will DOD's acquisition policy affect the planned incremental deployment strategy?

International Issues

How have other nations reacted to the new Administration's missile defense policy and why? What is the Bush Administration doing to address the concerns of U.S. allies and nations, such as Russia and China, who might feel threatened by U.S. missile defenses?

The final section of the report provides background information on the various parts of the Administration's proposed missile defense program. It includes program and budget data, and key technical challenges faced by the programs.

Missile Defense Prior to the Bush Administration

The United States has pursued the development of missile defenses for more than 50 years. Since the Reagan Strategic Defense Initiative (SDI) in 1985, the United States has spent almost $70 billion on missile defense programs and studies. Missile defense has proven to be a challenging and elusive endeavor. Moreover, the question of whether the United States should deploy extensive defenses to protect against ballistic missile attack has been one of the most divisive political and national security issues of this generation.

The demise of the Soviet Union and the debate over the emergence of ballistic missile threats[1] from other nations changed the nature of the debate. For many, concerns about nuclear stability between the United States and Russia have receded as the two nations have expanded their areas of cooperation and improved their relationship. Instead, many now focus on concerns about a possible attack from an adversary who possesses only a few missiles and may not be deterred by fear of U.S. retaliation. Without a missile defense capability, some argue, the United States itself may be deterred from using its conventional forces to protect U.S. allies and friends. Similarly, the United States might be unable to combat aggressive or provocative actions on the part of "rogue states" armed with chemical, biological, or nuclear capable ballistic missiles.[2] Even acquisition of ballistic missiles by terrorists is today part of the policy debate.

The Clinton Administration responded to this changing security environment by pursuing the development and deployment of defenses that would protect U.S. allies and forces in the field from attack by shorter and medium-range ballistic missiles (theater missile defense – TMD). It also sought to develop for deployment a limited system to protect U.S. territory from attack by longer-range ballistic missiles (national missile defense – NMD). Its plans for NMD would have conflicted with the terms of the 1972 Anti-ballistic Missile (ABM) Treaty with the Soviet Union, which limits the United States and Soviet Union (now Russia) to a single, land-based system for defense against long-range ballistic missiles.[3] The Administration sought to preserve the basic framework of the ABM Treaty by negotiating modifications that would have permitted the deployment of a limited, land-based NMD site in Alaska. The Clinton Administration decided, however, that it would not proceed to deploy the site after failures in the flight test program and other technical concerns raised questions about the readiness of the technology.

---

[1] This report does not examine the debate over threats from weapons of mass destruction and their means of delivery *per se*. Please see other CRS products, including: *Nuclear, Biological, and Chemical Weapons and Missiles: The Current Situation.* CRS Report RL30699, by Robert D. Shuey; *China's Proliferation of Weapons of Mass Destruction and missiles: Current Policy Issues.* CRS Issue Brief IB92056, by Shirley A. Kan.

[2] For example, see Kaplan, Lawrence F. Offensive Line: Why the Best Offense is a Good Missile Defense. *New Republic.* Mar. 12, 2001: 20-25.

[3] For a discussion of Treaty limits see the section: Treaty Limits and the Administration's Program, below.

Bush Administration's Proposed Approach

The Bush Administration sharply altered the debate over missile defense. In several speeches, President Bush indicated that he would pursue the development of technologies that could be deployed on land, at sea, and in space, and that would protect the United States, its allies, and its forces overseas from ballistic missile attacks on rogue nations. At the same time, the President stated that the United States would have to "move beyond the constraints" of the ABM Treaty. He emphasized that "Russia is not our enemy," and, therefore, Russia should not be concerned about U.S. deployment of missile defenses. Instead of seeking to modify the ABM Treaty so that the United States could deploy limited missile defenses, the President said "we need a new framework that allows us to build missile defenses to counter the different threats of today's world."[4]

The Administration began to outline the details of its plans for missile defenses in July 2001, after submitting its amended defense budget for FY2002 to Congress. In that budget, the Administration requested $8.3 billion for missile defense, an increase of $3.1 billion or 61 percent over the amount Congress funded for FY2001. The Administration stated that it would explore a broader range of technologies and basing modes, "including land, air, sea, and space-based capabilities that had been previously disregarded or inadequately explored." However, as is described in more detail later in this report (See Table 1), the Administration appears to have essentially increased funding evenly for each of the missile defense and sensor technologies already in the defense budget. From a funding and programmatic perspective, the Administration did not appear to give increased priority to any particular program or introduce any major new research directions for FY2002 beyond what the Clinton Administration was already pursuing, except to accelerate the process and integrate key components. A similar argument can be made with respect to the proposed FY 2003 missile defense budget of $7.8 billion.

In its missile defense program, the Bush Administration has eliminated distinctions between theater and national missile defenses (TMD and NMD). Instead, according to General Kadish, the director of the Missile Defense Agency (MDA) formerly the Ballistic Missile Defense Organization (BMDO), the Administration has "developed a research, development, and

---

[4] George W. Bush, Remarks on Missile Defense, National Defense University, May 1, 2001.

test program that focuses on missile defense as a single integrated BMD system." Furthermore, the objective of this program is to "aggressively evaluate and develop technologies for the integration of land, sea, air, or space-based platforms" and to develop and deploy a global system of "layered defenses, capable of intercepting missiles of any range at every stage of flight – boost, mid-course, and terminal.[5]

Administration officials have highlighted two primary benefits of layered defenses. First, layered defenses would seek to provide the United States with more than one opportunity to target an attacking missile, thus arguably increasing the chance of shooting it down. (A critique of the layered defense concept is outlined in the section on Technology and Other Challenges.)

Second, the layers could complicate an attacker's ability to defeat the overall system. This is because countermeasures, which are intended to confuse or overcome defenses that might be effective in one phase of a missile's flight might not work in other phases.

The Bush Administration has emphasized that its missile defense program will concentrate on "robust research and development" into a wide range of missile defense technologies. Unlike the Clinton Administration, the Bush Administration will not at this point identify an architecture that it will seek to deploy nor will it establish a schedule for the development and deployment of any particular system or element; but, a clear underlying objective is the early deployment of a defense against missiles aimed at U.S. territory. Because it has not identified the types of technologies or the numbers of interceptors and radars that it intends to deploy, the Administration will not provide any costs for the missile defense program or system. It emphasizes that cost estimates are premature under the new approach.

Administration officials have stated that this research and development effort is "designed to develop effective systems over time ... and to deploy that capability incrementally." The program envisions the deployment of "different combinations of sensors and weapons" when these technologies "are proven through robust testing." These technologies could then be

---

[5] The boost phase of a missile's flight occurs immediately after launch, and lasts for 3-5 minutes for long-range missiles and one or two minutes for short-range missiles; it is the powered portion of the flight. The midcourse portion occurs after boost, outside the atmosphere and, for long-range missiles, can last up to 20 minutes. The terminal phase occurs when a missile or warhead re-enters the atmosphere; it lasts less than a minute for short-range missiles and a minute or two for longer-range missiles.

replaced by more effective or advanced systems when they become available. This approach is called an evolutionary acquisition strategy. This strategy differs from the way in which most military acquisition programs occur. It will likely be the subject of increased scrutiny. An analysis of this strategy and some of its implications follows in a subsequent section of this report.

During congressional testimony, Deputy Secretary of Defense Wolfowitz stated repeatedly that the United States would not violate the ABM Treaty, but that the Treaty stood in the way of the Administrations' missile defense efforts. He noted that some of the tests or activities could "bump up" against the limits in the Treaty in "months' not years."[6] However, the Bush Administration also stated that the United States would have liked to reach an agreement with Russia that would allow these tests, and the eventual deployment of extensive missile defenses, to proceed without concern for the Treaty limits.

At a meeting in Italy in July, President Bush and Russia's President Putin agreed that the two nations would hold discussions that focused on both offensive weapons and defensive systems. Some interpreted this agreement to mean that the two nations would begin negotiations on new treaties that would limit offensive nuclear weapons and missile defenses. Administration officials stated clearly, however, that these were not negotiations, but consultations. They also stated that the Administration does not plan simply to seek modifications in the ABM Treaty, but also would not allow the Treaty to prevent research and development toward deployment even if that ultimately meant U.S. withdrawal from the Treaty.[7] Rather, the Bush Administration sought to convince Russia that the ABM Treaty is no longer relevant and that the two nations should agree to set it aside and replace it with a new framework for their relationship. According to some reports, the United States would share information about missile defense developments with Russia, but it would not accept any limits on research, development, or deployment of its systems. Russia, however, did not accept the U.S. approach, and, on December 1, 3001, President Bush announced that the United States would withdraw from the Treaty. Actual withdrawal could take place as early as June 13, 2002.

---

[6] U.S. Department of State. Cable on Missile Defense Policy. Published by the Carnegie Endowment for International Peace, July, 2001.

[7] In late August 2001, for example, John Bolton, Undersecretary of State for Arms Control and International Security, held out the possibility of invoking the withdrawal clause by November 2001 if "meaningful progress" with Russia was not achieved.

KEY ISSUES

ABM Treaty

Treaty Limits and the Administration's Program
The United States and the Soviet Union concluded and ratified the ABM Treaty in 1972[8] and agreed to a protocol that amended the Treaty in 1974.[9] The treaty, as amended bound each nation to these central provisions:

- "not to deploy ABM systems for a defense of the territory of its country, not to provide the base for such a defense, ... [or] for defense of an individual region except as provided in Article III" (Article I);

- "not to develop, test, or deploy ABM systems or components which are sea-based, air-based, space-based, or mobile land-based" (Article V);

- "not to give missiles, launchers, or radars, other than ABM interceptor missiles, ABM launchers, or ABM radars, capabilities to counter strategic ballistic missiles or their elements in flight trajectory, and not to test them in an ABM mode" (Article VI);

- "not to deploy in the future radars for early warning of strategic ballistic missile attack except at locations along the periphery of its national territory and oriented outward" (Article VI); and

- "not to transfer to other States, and not to deploy outside its national territory, ABM systems of their components limited by this Treaty" (Article IX).

The Treaty does not bar the Parties from developing, testing, and deploying a fixed land-based ABM system. But it allows the deployment of such a system only around each nation's capital or around one ICBM complex (Article III). (The USSR chose to deploy its system around

---
[8] TIAS 7503; 23 UST 3435 (1972).
[9] TIAS 8276; 27 UT 1645 (1976).

Moscow, while the United States chose to defend an ICBM complex in North Dakota. But the United States dismantled[10] its system within a few months.) Moreover, the Treaty also allows the Parties to continue to test and improve their fixed land-based ABM systems and components. But it limits each Party to a maximum of 15 ABM launchers at its test ranges and requires further agreement between the Parties for the establishment of new test ranges (Article IV).

According to Administration officials, the Bush Administration developed its missile defense program without consideration for the limits and provisions in the ABM treaty. In testimony before the Senate Armed Services Committee, Deputy Secretary of Defense Paul Wolfowitz stated that the Administration sought to develop "the most capable possible defense" which would, at some point – sooner, rather than later – encounter the constraints of the ABM Treaty." The Administration has also asserted that it did not design any tests of its planned missile defense technologies "solely to exceed treaty constraints." But it went on to state that there was no intent to design tests or activities to conform to, or stay within, the confines of the Treaty.[11]

Several elements of the Administration's missile defense plan are in clear contrast to the provisions in the Treaty. First, the deployment of a defense designed to protect the entire United States from ballistic missile attack could be seen as inconsistent with the Treaty's ban on the deployment of ABM systems for the defense of the nation's territory. Even if the defense were limited in its numbers of interceptors and radars, so that it could not completely protect U.S. territory from a large attack, the system could still be seen as a base for the defense of the entire territory. Furthermore, the deployment of a layered defense that uses land-based, sea-based, and space-based components is inconsistent with the Treaty's ban on the deployment of sea-based, space-based, and mobile land-based ABM components. And finally, some of the tests planned for the coming year could conflict with the Treaty's ban on testing non-ABM systems in an ABM mode. The Bush Administration does not deny the existence of these potential conflicts; instead, they serve as evidence of the Administration's view that the United States has to move beyond the constraints in the ABM Treaty to provide an effective defense of the entire nation, its allies, and its forces overseas.

---

[10] Technically, Congress withdrew funding support for operating the ABM complex and the Army consequently removed the interceptor missiles, personnel, and other hardware, thus placing the site in caretaker status where it remains today.

[11] U.S. Department of State. Cable on Missile Defense Policy. Published by the Carnegie Endowment for International Peace, July, 2001. p. 3.

Compliance Questions

The Bush Administration has publicly identified three events that could raise questions about U.S. compliance with the ABM Treaty.[12] These include initial construction activities on a new test site at Ft. Greely in Alaska, a systems integration test combining data from ABM and non-AMB radars, and the use of an Aegis Spy-1 radar to track an ICBM target during a missile defense test. The compliance issues involved with these plans are complex, in part because the Treaty does not contain precise definitions of the activities in question.

The first of these events raises questions because of the location and intent of the site in Alaska; the latter two raise questions about the capabilities of non-ABM radars to perform ABM missions and the Treaty's prohibition on testing them "in an ABM mode." The ABM Treaty does not include a definition of tested in an AMB mode. However, at the time it was concluded in 1972, the U.S. delegation made a unilateral statement describing its understanding of the meaning of "tested in an ABM" mode. The Soviet Union neither joined nor objected to this U.S. unilateral interpretation. The United States stated that:

> ... we note that we would consider a launcher, missile, or radar to be "tested in an AMB mode" if, for example, any of the following events occur: (1) a launcher is used to launch an ABM interceptor missile, (2) an interceptor missile is flight tested against a target vehicle which has a flight trajectory with characteristics of a strategic ballistic missile flight trajectory, or is flight tested in conjunction with the test of an ABM interceptor missile or an ABM radar at the same test range, or is flight tested to an altitude inconsistent with interception of targets against which air defenses are deployed, (3) a radar makes measurements on a cooperative target vehicle of the kind referred to in item (2) above during the reentry portion of its trajectory or makes measurements in conjunction with the test of an ABM interceptor missile or an ABM radar at the same test range.[13]

In 1978 the United States and Soviet Union adopted a definition of "tested in an ABM mode" in the SCC that, in part, echoes this unilateral

---

[12] The Senate Armed Services Committee included a provision in its version of the Defense Authorization Bill that would require congressional approval before funds could be spent on activities that might violate the ABM Treaty.

[13] 23 UST 3460-61.

statement. They agreed that a component tested in an ABM mode would include an ABM:

- launcher that has been used to launch an ABM interceptor missile
- interceptor missile that has either been launched from an ABM launcher and guided by an ABM radar or that has intercepted a strategic ballistic missile in flight trajectory while guided by an ABM radar
- radar that has tracked a strategic ballistic missile in flight trajectory and guided an interceptor missile toward it.[14]

Further clarification was sought during the 1990s when the United States and Russia negotiated two Agreed Statements on Demarcation that sought to define the difference between ABM and TMD systems, and could help distinguish whether a TMD system had been tested "in an ABM mode." These agreements do not limit the capabilities of TMD interceptors, but they define an ABM target missile as one that has a range greater than 3,500 kilometers and a speed greater than 5 kilometers per second. If TMD systems are tested against targets with these capabilities, they would be considered to be "tested in an ABM mode" or ABM systems subject to the limits in the Treaty. The Clinton Administration had agreed to consider these statements to be amendments to the Treaty, even though it viewed them as simple clarifications, and to submit these statements to the Senate for advice and consent. But it had not done so by the end of its term.

Midcourse Test Bed: Ft. Greely, Alaska Site

The Administration intends to construct a new test bed for its missile defense program that includes two sites in Alaska. This test bed would include 5 silos that could launch interceptor missiles from Ft. Greely and two silos at Kodiak Island that could launch interceptors or target missiles. The test bed would also use at least three large phased-array radars – an upgraded Cobra Dane radar at Shemya, Alaska, an upgraded radar at Beale Air Force Base in California, and a new X-Band radar that would be constructed in the mid-Pacific. Preliminary efforts to clear trees and prepare roads at the Ft. Greely Army base are underway, but construction of facilities and silos would not begin until the weather clears in the Spring of 2002.[15]

---

[14] SCC, *Agreed Statement of November 1, 1978*.
[15] A $9 million contract was awarded on Aug. 17, 2001, to a native Alaskan Company (Aglaq Construction Enterprises) for clearing trees, grading the site, and installing preliminary utilities and road structures.

According to the Administration, this new test bed would achieve several objectives. It would allow the testing of missile defense interceptors at different trajectories, which could provide more realistic assessments of their capabilities; it would allow tests with more complex engagement scenarios, including those that would allow the launch of multiple interceptors at incoming targets; it would allow DOD to practice operations and maintenance activities and assess how Arctic conditions might affect system components; and it might provide a rudimentary operational capability by 2004 if emerging threats required such a system.

An ABM system in Alaska (i.e., one designed to intercept long-range ballistic missiles) is not permitted under the terms of the ABM Treaty. The Treaty permits such a site around Washington, D.C. or within a certain specified area containing ICBM silos. But the Treaty permits the construction of a test facility in a location such as Alaska. In general, the Treaty allows the Parties to continue to test and improve their fixed land-based ABM systems and components at current *or additionally agreed* test ranges," as long as there are no more than 15 ABM launchers at its test ranges. In 1978, in an Agreed Statement negotiated in the SCC, the Parties agreed that additional test ranges could be established without further negotiation as long as their establishment was consistent with the objectives and provisions of the Treaty" and, in particular, did not violate Article I, which includes the prohibition on defenses that could provide the base for a national defense.

Because the Administration has stated that the facilities in Alaska could become a rudimentary ICBM defense capability, their planned construction raised compliance questions. It is not clear at what point, however, construction would constitute a violation. The Treaty does not define "construction" or indicate when in the construction process a violation would occur. Lawyers in the Clinton Administration sought to address this compliance question in support of the possibility that the President would authorize construction of an ABM radar in Shemya, Alaska.[16] Most experts agree that early activities, such as clearing and grading land, would not violate the treaty because these activities could precede any type of construction activity. But the lawyers in the Clinton Administration and outside experts never agreed on when some construction activities, such as

---

[16] Sirak, Michael C. U.S. Considers Impact of Constructions Schedule on NMD Decision. *Inside the Army.* May 8, 2000, p. 1.

excavation or the pouring of concrete in support of an ABM site, would violate the Treaty.

Some Russian officials and other arms control advocates have stated that they would consider any ground-breaking activities in Alaska a violation of the Treaty. And, even if the early activities were only a "sign" of U.S. intentions to violate the Treaty, the pouring of concrete into silos would certainly be a violation because "pouring concrete is an irreversible operation."[17] This question, however, is no longer relevant because the Bush Administration announced that the United States will withdraw from the Treaty in June 2002, as construction on the silos begins.

PAC-3 System Integration Test

The Pentagon planned a test of the Patriot PAC-3 system in February 2002 that could have raised questions about the ABM Treaty's ban on testing non-ABM systems in an ABM mode. During this test, three targets were to be tracked by radars associated with Aegis, Patriot PAC-3, and THAAD systems. According to a fact sheet provided to the Senate Armed Services Committee by BMDO, an ABM radar at the Kwajalein Missile Range was going to also track each target. This radar was not going to communicate with the other radars, so this tracking information would not be used to help the PAC-3 system intercept its target.

However, according to BMDO, the data collected by the ABM radar would support all TMD programs by providing information about how the interceptors and the target missiles behave. Because ABM and non-ABM radars would operate a the same time, and track the same objects, the non-ABM radars could be considered to be "tested in an ABM mode," according to the unilateral interpretation offered by the United States in 1972. The details of the test, though, could affect the determination of whether or not it is consistent with the ABM Treaty. This test took place on February 16, 2001, with two of the three planned intercepts failing to hit their targets.

During the 1980s, however, the United States indicated that it *did* consider concurrent testing of ABM and non-ABM radars to be a violation of the ABM Treaty. In several Compliance Reports that Presidents Reagan and Bush submitted to Congress, the United States expressed concerns about Soviet tests that operated AMB radars and non-ABM, air-defense radars concurrently. The reports state clearly that the United States had pursued the quoted definitions of "tested in an ABM mode" precisely so that the Treaty

---

[17] Baker, Peter. Russia Says Alaska Test Site Violates ABM Treaty. Washington Post, July 20, 2001. p. A23.

would constrain the Soviet Union's ability to upgrade its air-defense systems to have an ABM capability.[18]

Aegis Spy-1 Tracking an ICBM Test[19]

According to information provided to the Senate Armed Services Committee, BMDO plans to use an Aegis Spy-1 radar to track an ICBM target missile after its launch from Vandenberg Air Force Base during a missile defense intercept attempt from the Kwajalein Missile Range. Initially, this event was to occur during IFT-7 (Integrated Flight Test-7), which was scheduled for October 2001. For technical reasons, this test was delayed until later. Although the Aegis radar may be connected to the test's command and control system, its data reportedly would not be used in the intercept attempt. However, this test would allow BMDO to assess the ability of an Aegis radar to track ICBM-range targets and to formulate options for the further development of Aegis radars. BMDO has also indicated that, in the future, it might conduct other tests that integrate Aegis Spy-1 radars into ABM tests and operate them at the ABM Test range (both at Kwajalein and at the new Ft. Greely site).

The Aegis Spy-1 radar is a part of the Navy's air defense system, and is being considered to assist in a proposed naval short-range missile defense system. The Aegis radar is not an ABM radar, but could be considered to be tested in an ABM mode if it tracks an ICBM-range target, especially during an interceptor test. However, details of the test could affect the determination about its compliance with the Treaty and the foregoing interpretations. Furthermore, the statements quoted above are not a part of the formal text of the Treaty. Hence, it is not clear that the United States would be in violation of the Treaty if it conducted a test that was inconsistent with these statements.

In late October 2001, Secretary of Defense Rumsfeld stated that this test had been delayed because there were concerns among some in the Pentagon that it could violate the ABM Treaty. The President and others in his Administration have stated that the United States would not violate the Treaty, but would seek Russia's approval or would withdraw from the Treaty if necessary. When observers highlighted information indicating that the

---

[18] See, for example, U.S. Arms Control and Disarmament Agency. Soviet Noncompliance with Arms Control Agreements. September 27, 1990. pp. 14-16.

[19] The summary here, and in the next two sections, is derived from point papers that BMDO provided to the Senate Armed Services Committee with the prepared testimony of Deputy Secretary of Defense Wolfowitz on July 17, 2001.

Ballistic Missile Defense Organization had delayed the test for technical reasons, not treaty reasons, Secretary Rumsfeld agreed, but stated that the concerns about the Treaty would eliminate the Aegis portion of the test when the flight occurred later in the year. A test that included tracking with an Aegis radar now is not scheduled to occur until Spring 2002. Some observers noted that Secretary Rumsfeld may have highlighted the Treaty implications of the test, in part, to indicate that the ABM Treaty had already affected the Administration's missile defense plan and to support arguments that the United States needed to withdraw from the Treaty soon.

The Department of Defense Compliance Review Group (CRG) has evaluated these three activities and sent its preliminary findings to Deputy Secretary Wolfowitz. Reports indicate that it did find the use of the Aegis Spy-1 radar to track an ICBM intercept test to be in violation of the Treaty. According to the Pentagon, Deputy Secretary Wolfowitz could weigh a number of options to address the concerns, from delaying the activity in question to opening a broader discussion within the government's interagency process to determine how to proceed.[20] A broader interagency review may also address questions about the interpretation of the Treaty and its negotiating record. Construction activities scheduled for spring 2002 in Alaska may be viewed by Administration officials as driving the need to invoke the requisite 6-month withdrawal notice. Others might suggest this is part of a strategy to discourage the Russians from prolonged negotiations.

The Senate Armed Services Committee included a provision, in its version of the FY2002 Defense Authorization Bill, (S. 1416), that would have required approval by a joint resolution of Congress before any funds could be spent on activities that would violate the ABM Treaty. The Republican Members of the Committee strongly opposed the provision and Secretary of Defense Rumsfeld suggested that it could lead to a Presidential veto of the Defense Authorization Bill. In the wake of the attacks on the World Trade Center and Pentagon, and in the interest of prompt passage of the Defense Authorization Bill, Senate leaders agreed to remove the provision from the Bill. At the time, Senator Levin, Chairman of the Armed Services Committee, stated that he would introduce free-standing legislation to achieve this objective.

---

[20] Department of Defense, News Briefing. Rear Adm. Craig R. Quigley. July 31, 2001.

Legal Status and Withdrawal

On December 13, 2001, President Bush announced that he had given notice to Russia's President Putin that the United States would withdraw from the ABM Treaty; with the 6-months notice required by the Treaty, this withdrawal would take effect in June 2002. The United States had sought to reach a cooperative solution with Russia, presumably so that Russia would either allow unlimited missile defense tests or agree to "set aside" the Treaty with the United States (this is discussed in more detail below). But these discussions failed to product an agreement.

Article XV of the Treaty states that either party can withdraw "if it decides that extraordinary events related to the subject matter of this Treaty have jeopardized its supreme interests" (Article XV). Withdrawal requires six-months advance notice that includes a statement of the events that have necessitated withdrawal. In the past, Presidents have often given notices of withdrawal from various treaties on their own authority without the participation of either the Senate or the Congress as a whole. But some analysts argue that withdrawal from a treaty of this importance requires Senate or Congressional authorization.[21] The Administration did not seek congressional approval, but simply informed members of its intention to withdraw.

Some analysts, and some members of Congress, argue that the Administration did not need to withdraw from the ABM Treaty. They argue instead that the ABM Treaty ceased to be in force after the demise of the Soviet Union. This view is based, in part, on the contention that international law affords the successor states of the Soviet Union a "clean slate" with respect to its treaty rights and obligations. It is based as well on the contention that key provisions of the Treaty can no longer be performed because the treaty can no longer be applied to the entire territory of the former Soviet Union and because a bilateral treaty cannot automatically be converted into a multilateral treaty. Changes in a treaty that are that dramatic, it is said, mean that the old treaty no longer exists. Others argue, however, that international law, as well as all of the (former Soviet) states that are relevant to the ABM Treaty, recognize a continuity of treaty obligations for the successor states of the Soviet Union and particularly its arms control treaties, that it is a constitutional prerogative of the Executive

---

[21] For a description of the variety of ways in which the United States has terminated treaties in the past, see the Congressional Research Service, *Treaties and Other International Agreements: The Role of the United States Senate*, (S. Comm. Print 106-71) (January, 2001), pp. 198-208.

Branch to decide whether particular treaties remain in force, and that necessary changes to the ABM Treaty can be made either through agreements negotiated by the Executive Branch or by amendments subject to the advice and consent of the Senate.

The first Bush Administration and the Clinton Administration operated as if the ABM Treaty remained in force. The current Bush Administration did the same, hence it gave notice of the U.S. withdrawal from the Treaty to eliminate constraints that would impinge on planned U.S. missile defense tests. To make clear which of the new states succeeded to the rights and obligations of the Soviet Union under the Treaty, the Clinton Administration negotiated a Memorandum of Understanding on Succession (MOUS) that designated not only Russia but also Belarus, Kazakhstan, and the Ukraine as the successor states. Some in Congress argued that this MOU was an amendment to the Treaty and requires that it be submitted to the Senate for advice and consent. The Clinton Administration did not do so before it left office, however, because it feared it would be defeated. Instead, the Administration stated that it would assume Russia was the successor to the Soviet Union, as it was in a significant number of other arms control, tax, and trade treaties.

Discussions with Russia

When they met after the G-8 summit in Genoa, Italy in late July 2001, Presidents Bush and Putin agreed that the two nations would resume discussions on offensive weapons and missile defenses. These discussions began with consultations in Washington in early August, during which time Pentagon officials provided the visiting Russians with detailed descriptions of its missile defense plans and technologies, meetings between Secretary of Defense Rumsfeld and President Putin and Minister of Defense Ivanov in mid-August and further discussions between high-ranking officials later in August and September.[22]

The Bush Administration did not view these discussions as the opening round in a formal negotiating process that might produce a new treaty limiting offensive nuclear weapons or missile defenses. The President and officials in his Administration have often said, "Russia is not our enemy," and that, in the absence of an adversarial relationship, formal arms control agreements are no longer needed to manage the relationship between the two nations. Instead, some analysts suggest that the United States may be seeking

---

[22] U.S.-Russian Defense Officials Meet. *New York Times* on the Web. August 8, 2001.

a more informal process where the two sides simply inform each other of their plans and programs.[23] Furthermore, the United States would have liked Russia to agree to set aside the ABM Treaty, or to have both parties withdraw from it together, so that the United States could proceed with missile defense. The Administration did not intend to let these talks drag on or delay its missile defense plans. President Bush states that, if the two sides could not soon reach an agreement to set the Treaty aside together, the United States would withdraw and deploy defenses.[24] In meetings with Russian officials, Undersecretary of State John Bolton seemed to indicate that time would run out in November, when Presidents Bush and Putin were scheduled to meet in Texas. Other Administration officials denied the existence of a firm deadline, but President Bush stated that the United States would withdraw from the ABM Treaty according to our own timetable.

Russia, on the other hand, would prefer to keep some form of Treaty regime in place. It acknowledges that the world has changed and that the relationship with the United States has changed, but it continues to place a value on the predictability and formality offered by arms control agreements. Reports indicate that it might have been willing to permit more extensive testing of missile defense systems, and to relax the definitions in the Agreed Statements on Demarcation to that the United States could test systems designed to destroy shorter-range missiles against a wider range of targets. But, even if it may now be willing to modify the ABM Treaty so that the United States can conduct these tests, it does not favor an environment in which the United States can deploy missile defenses without limitations.

In spite of these differences, the two sides seemed to reach some common ground in September and October, 2001, in preparation for the summit in Washington and Crawford in mid-November. Reports in the weeks before the meeting indicated that the United States was willing to remain a party to the ABM Treaty, and delay its presumed withdrawal until it planned to deploy missile defenses, as long as Russia was willing to permit the United States to conduct the testing program it deemed necessary. Some analysts assumed this agreement would produce formal amendments to the ABM Treaty, but the Administration apparently sought a less formal agreement where Russia would quietly accept the U.S. testing program in exchange for a delay in the U.S. withdrawal from the Treaty.

---

[23] Gordon, Michael. White House Finding Putin a Friend Indeed. *New York Times*. July 23, 2001. p. 1.
[24] Sammon, Bill. Bush Won't Let ABM Treaty Derail Missile Defense. *Washington Times*, July 24, 2001. p. 1.

However, Presidents Bush and Putin did not announce this type of agreement after their meetings in Washington and Crawford. Instead, they agreed that they would continue to disagree about their differences over the ABM Treaty. President Putin did indicate that he understood U.S. concerns about emerging threats and he stated that differences over the ABM Treaty should not lead to a breakdown in the new, cooperative relationship between the two nations. Some analysts interpreted these comments to mean that Russia might still turn a blind eye if the United States conducted tests that were inconsistent with the ABM Treaty, even in the absence of a formal agreement. Nevertheless, because these tests scheduled to occur and construction at the Fort Greeley site should begin before the middle of 2002, the Bush Administration had to decide how to proceed. These events reportedly led the President to announce, on December 13, that the United States would withdraw from the Treaty.

BUDGET AND PROGRAM

Budget Allocation and Program Restructuring

The missile defense program was restructured effective Oct. 1, 2002 – the new fiscal year. Some programs were supposed to be moved to the military services; BMDO argued these were more mature programs that were developed out of an air defense capability and should be returned to the services for advanced development and acquisition.[25] In the end, Congress did not authorize these program transfers to the services. Other programs were moved from the Air Force to BMDO and now the MDA.

The restructuring had been proposed for several reasons. The principal ones were that BMDO wanted to focus primarily on the various phases of a ballistic missile's flight trajectory (as opposed to its range – theater vs. long-range – which was the case previously), and take advantage of the concept of layered defense. The layered defense concept is designed to employ multiple missile defenses at various portions of an attacking missile's flight to enhance the probability of its destruction. This concept is examined in more detail later. The new, major program elements (which are also detailed more fully in the final section of this report) within BMDO are:

---

[25] These include the Patriot PAC-3/MEADS program, which were to be run by the Army, and the Navy Area Defense program (since cancelled).

- **Boost Defense Segment,** which includes Air-Based Boost (also known as the Air Force Airborne Laser, or ABL) and Space-Based Boost (also known as the Air Force Space Based Laser Experiment and the BMDO Space-Based laser Experiment);

- **Midcourse Defense Segment,** which includes Ground-Based Midcourse (also known as the BMDO National Missile Defense, or NMD, and Sea-Based Midcourse (also known as the BMDO Navy Theater Wide, or NTW);

- **Terminal Defense Segment,** which includes Ground-Based Terminal (also known as the Army Theater High Altitude Area Defense, or THAAD), and the Israeli Arrow Deployability Program (ADP); and

- **Sensors Segment** – includes the Space Sensor (also known as the Space-Based Infrared System-Low, or SBIRS-L) and International cooperation (known also as the Russian-American Observation Satellite, or RAMOS – a joint, non-missile defense program).

The Bush Administration requested $8.3 billion for missile defense in FY2002, an increase of about 61 percent above that approved by Congress for FY2001. The Administration argued this increase was necessary to enhance previously inadequately funded missile defense programs, accelerate near-term missile defense options, allow for more realistic testing of missile defense elements, and explore new missile defense concepts. The Administration and BMDO further argued that each missile defense program was carefully assessed and funding for each program was based on objective needs for FY2002.

A budgetary analysis, however, suggests that the percentage share of the budget total devoted to each major program element (e.g., boost,[26] midcourse,[27] terminal,[28] sensors,[29] BMD Technology,[30] and headquarters[31]) as a function of the total missile defense budget, is virtually identical to that

---

[26] Includes: boost defense segment, Airborne Laser, and Space-based laser.
[27] Includes: BMD midcourse, NMD, and NTW.
[28] Includes: BMD terminal segment, Patriot PAC-3, MEADS, NAD, THAAD.
[29] Includes: BMD sensors, SBIRS-L, International Cooperation.
[30] Includes: BMD segment, BMD technology, BMD support and technology.
[31] Includes: BMD headquarters.

approved by Congress for FY2001. (This does not include the FY2001 Supplemental, which would change these percentages marginally.) See Table 1.[32] The only apparent difference between the two is the large increase in funding for the program elements.

---

[32] Comparisons reflect the April estimate for FY2001 and the FY2002 Amended budget request; effects of the FY2001 supplemental appropriations are not included. Funding includes RDT&E, procurement, and military construction.

Table 1. Changes in Missile Defense Funding FY 2001 vs. FY2002[33]
(millions of dollars or percent)

Program Elements	FY2001 Estimated Funding	FY2002 Amended Budget Funding	FY2002 Enacted	FY2001 Share of Total	FY2002 Enacted Share of Total	FY2002 Enacted vs. FY2001 % Change
Terminal	1,399.4	2,240.9	1,975.5	27%	26%	41%
Midcourse	2,411.3	3,940.5	3,820.5	47%	49%	58%
Boost	304.0	685.4	609.4	6%	8%	100%
Sensors	274.2	495.6	340.6	5%	4%	24%
MBD Technology	745.3	912.5	960.2	15%	12%	29%
Headquarters	4.7	34.3	34.4	0%	0%	627%
TOTAL	5,139.0	8,309.3	7,740.6	100%	100%	51%

[33] Adapted from Table 7 in: Appropriations and Authorization for FY2002: Defense, CRS Report RL31005, August 9, 2001, coordinated by Amy Belasco, Mary Tyszkiewicz, and Stephen Daggett.

More recently, the Pentagon announced the redesignation of BMDO as the Missile Defense Agency (MDA). Elevating BMDO to agency status is designed to demonstrate the national priority and mission emphasis on missile defense. The overall objectives for missile defense include: establishing a single program to develop an integrated missile defense system; assigning the best personnel to this effort, and applying a capability-based requirements process for missile defense, according to the Department of Defense. The MDA will develop the missile defense system and baseline its capability and configuration. The military services will procure the system and provide for operations and support.

The $3.1 billion increase received considerable congressional attention, especially prior to the events of September 2001. Although some missile defense advocates may have questioned its adequacy, many supported the Administration's efforts to advance missile defense development and possible deployment as quickly as possible, in part due to perceived, near-term threats from weapons of mass destruction and their means of delivery. Others, however, were beginning to question the ability of the Defense Department and defense contractors to absorb such large increases in missile defense spending in a single year. Still others questioned the propriety of such large Program Elements (e.g., $3.94 billion for the Midcourse PE and $2.2 billion for the Terminal PE).

The Senate Armed Services Committee, in its version of the FY2002 Defense Authorization Bill (S. 1416), eliminated $1.3 billion of the requested funding for ballistic missile defense. In its report, the Committee argued that this funding was "poorly justified and would be better used elsewhere in the Department." The Committee also questioned the Administration's reorganization of the program elements for missile defense, arguing that the consolidation of programs would allow for the easy transfer of funds without congressional oversight. It allowed the change to stand, but it required that the Administration submit detailed reports outlining their annual plans for missile defense spending.

A major practical effect of this restructuring is that it eliminates the distinction between national (i.e., defenses designed to destroy long-range missiles or warheads) and theater missile defense (i.e., defenses designed to destroy short- and medium-range missiles or warheads). The Administration argues such distinctions serve little purpose and actually encumber meaningful development of layered missile defenses.

Critics charge that by blurring these distinctions at least two important concerns are raised. First, distinctions between prohibited NMD activities under the ABM Treaty are now blurred with permitted TMD activities; the Treaty becomes less meaningful. Second, more successful TMD intercept tests are now mixed in with far more ambiguous NMD test activities, leading to inferences about NMD success that are more ambiguous.

Defense Budget Competition

Increased funding for missile defense also will likely intensify already-keen competition within the Defense Department for scarce resources. In addition to missile defense, the Pentagon is facing rising funding demands for many other priorities, including military operations in response to the September 11, 2001 terrorist attacks; rapidly rising costs for personnel pay and benefits; particularly health care; continued, apparently unabated growth in the cost of operation and maintenance of equipment and facilities; maintenance, refurbishment and replacement of buildings and facilities; and procurement of new weapons and equipment, both to "recapitalize" existing weapons procured primarily in prior years and to "transform" the force with advanced intelligence, surveillance, and communications equipment, new munitions, and other programs. The Administration is also expanding efforts in areas such as homeland defense (especially after September 11, 2002), cyberwarfare, and defense against cruise missiles.

Supporters of DoD programs other than missile defense – including, by some accounts, some senior leaders within the military services – are concerned that the Administration's missile-defense plan might be financed at the expense of other important DoD programs. Last year, some critics of the Administration's proposal to increase funding for missile defense proposed reducing the Administration's FY2002 funding request for missile defense and applying the freed-up funding to other programs, such as readiness-related programs, procurement programs for aircraft, ships, and ground-combat equipment, or emerging DoD priorities such as homeland defense, counterterrorism, or cyberwarfare. After September 11, these contentious proposals were shelved. Instead, the Senate included a provision in its version of the FY2002 defense authorization bill (S. 1438) that permitted the President to use up to $1.3 billion of missile defense funds to combat terrorism, and that measure was incorporated into the conference agreement on the authorization. The final appropriations bill, however, did not include such a provision.

This year, despite large proposed increases on overall defense spending, some lawmakers on the congressional defense committees have complained that the proposed level of funding for some programs is inadequate. The most vocal complaints have come from Members of Congress from shipbuilding states. The Navy is requesting only give new ships in FY2003 and has delayed shipbuilding plans in future years, including, notably the planned production start of the next aircraft carrier. Only at the very end of the FY2003-2007 give-year Pentagon plan will projected ship purchases reach the rate of 8 to 10 ships per year needed, in principle, to maintain a Navy of 300 ships with an average service life of 35 years (i.e., 300 ships divided by 35 years per ship = 8.6 new ships per year needed to sustain the fleet).

Similarly, production rates for fighter aircraft and helicopters are not near sustaining levels, studies persistently point to airlift shortfalls, the Army has proposed terminating 18 small programs, some of which are popular in Congress, and some legislators complain that munitions production remains inadequate, despite a substantial boost in the budget, pointing out that stockpiles have been drained by a relatively small war in Afghanistan. meanwhile, each of the military services wants an increase in the number of active duty personnel to cope with the ongoing pace of operations. The Army is looking for the largest increment, seeking to add as many as 40,000 troops to the 480,000 now in service.

As a result, the funding priority that the Administration has given to missile defense may again be a matter of some debate in Congress. Potential issues for Congress include the following:

- Does the Administration's proposed FY2003 level of missile defense funding come at the expense of other equal- or higher-priority defense DoD programs? If so, what are these programs, and should FY2003 funding be shifted from missile defense into these program?

- What is the risk in future years that funding demands for missile defense will crowd out funding demands for other important DoD programs, particularly procurement programs? How well can this risk be calculated when the potential long-term costs of the missile defense program cannot be estimated?

- If reductions elsewhere in the defense budget may be needed to finance missile defense, which programs should be reduced?

- What effect will the Administration's proposed spiral acquisition strategy – and the resultant inability to provide estimates of the potential longer term costs of the missile-defense program – have on DoD's ability to create a reliable Future Years Defense Plan (FYDP) and to conduct other long-range program and budget planning? What effect, if any, will this have on Congress' ability to rely on the FYDP to understand the potential composition of the defense budget in future years?

TECHNICAL ISSUES AND ACQUISITION STRATEGY

Technology and Other Challenges

Hit-to-Kill

The concept of kinetic kill or hit-to-kill has been a primary focus of the missile defense program since the conception of the SDI in the early 1980s. previously, the United States pursued missile defense concepts that employed nuclear weapons as interceptors. More conventional explosive warheads were used to develop the PAC-2 system used in the Persian Gulf War against Iraqi Scud missiles. Advanced and exotic concepts, such as various lasers, were largely deemed impractical during the late 1980s and early 1990s.

A kinetic kill interceptor would seek to destroy its intended target through a direct collision at relatively high speeds. The force of the impact would then destroy the attacking missile or warhead, render it inoperable, or divert it from its intended target. With such an approach, a near-miss has the same practical affect as a large distance miss – the target is not destroyed.

Kinetic kill as a concept for destroying short- and medium-range ballistic missiles appears to be in the process of proving itself. After a string of failed intercept tests, the THAAD program finally began a series of successful tests. Barring major, unforeseen technical or engineering problems, it appears that a kinetic kill warhead for THAAD can e developed. The same is true of the PAC-3 system. The next generation Patriot interceptor seems to be proving the concept of kinetic kill for short-range missile defenses, despite the most recent test failures in February 2002.

The key question remaining, however, centers around levels of effectiveness, particularly in wartime. Under test-range conditions, most military systems perform better than they do in an operational environment. The Patriot system used in Desert Storm is a notable example. Prior to the war, Patriot successfully intercepted 17 of 17 very different targets under a variety of test range conditions. Patriot encountered a vastly different operational environment when deployed, and its success or failure during the war is still debatable, and according to experts, probably ultimately unknowable.

Kinetic kill as a concept for destroying long-range ballistic missiles is even more problematic at this stage. There is no unambiguous, empirical evidence to support the contention that kinetic kill for ICBM defense will work. Missile defense advocates argue that since the mid-1980s, a string of such tests have occurred with varying degrees of success; some have failed to achieve interception, while others were deemed successful.'

But in almost every case, post-test doubts have been raised. Critics have charged that test results over the past two decades have been exaggerated y false claims of success and promises of performance that later proved false. Many tests were proven to have had their targets significantly enhanced to ensure the likelihood of success.

Some missile defense advocates say this may be true. But kinetic kill for ICBM defense is comparable to where kinetic kill was for systems such as PAC-3 several years ago. They maintain, therefore, that continued development, and especially more realistic testing, is needed to ensure that the kinetic kill concept for long-range missiles can eventually be deployed.

Layered Defenses

The concept of layered defense, which dates back to at least the 1960s, and was developed more systematically in the 1980s, envisions deploying several missile defense systems, each designed to intercept an attacking missile or warhead at a different stage of its flight trajectory. The concept arguably would allow for multiple intercept opportunities. Although this presents the possibility that one element of the system may not work as intended, proponents argue that multiple intercept opportunities significantly *increase* the chance that an attacking missile or warhead will be destroyed.

Proponents of layered defenses argue that each layer is able to attack a different vulnerability of the attacking ballistic missile and that, because each layer is statistically independent of every other layer, the probability of a warhead getting through all of the layers (1 to N) can be given by a simple multiplication of the probabilities of surviving each independent attack.[34] This analysis would readily lead to a conclusion that a defense with three layers, for example, might let extremely few missiles or warheads get through.

Other analysts, however, would argue that this is a wrong conclusion. In the first place, there is no empirical evidence of an air defense system with a probability of intercept (P_i) much greater than about 30 percent (or 0.3). So one might conclude more realistically that the probability that an attacking missile or warhead will survive is closer to 34 percent.[35] Moreover, it is argued,[36] even if one assumes that each layer *is* 90 percent effective, the layered defense model fails because the layers are *not* statistically independent for at least two reasons:

- Each attacking warhead or missile must encounter each of the layers in order, so the performance of one layer will affect the performance of the next layer and so on. For example, if the first layer underperforms because some countermeasure is unexpectedly successful, then the second layer will be required to deal with more simultaneous targets than expected; if one missile or warhead avoids interception, that may mean that circumstances are favorable for the next missile to get through also. Even if each layer is over designed by a factor of about 2, failure of one layer can still lead to saturation of the next. For example, if we expect the terminal layer to have to handle ten warheads, we might design it to handle 20, but if earlier layers then fail so that the terminal layer is presented with 30 targets, at least ten warheads will get through to their intended destination even if the terminal layer works perfectly. The failure of an early layer would thus result in the collapse of the missile defense system: the layered 'pyramid' defense is balanced on its vertex, rather than set firmly on its base.

---

[34] For example, suppose that a missile defense system consists of three independent layers, each with a kill probability of 90%. Then the probability of surviving each layer is 10 percent (or 0.10), and the probability of surviving all three layers is 0.10 x 0.10 x 0.10 = 0.001. In other words, in such a system only one missile in a thousand will get through.

[35] 0.7 x 0l7 x 0.7 = 0.343; that is, 34% of the missiles or warheads would survive this layered missile defense system.

[36] A critique of the layered defense concept is developed by: Zimmerman, Peter D. Pork Bellies and SDI. *Foreign Policy* (Summer 1987): 76-87.

- Until a layered defense has been tested under realistic conditions, when it must engage warheads nearly simultaneously in each layer, it is unrealistic for defense planners to assume that there are no problems of command and control among the layers, and that unknown variables do not operate to degrade the system in unpredicted ways. Such a test would be expensive and difficult to achieve, requiring the multiple simultaneous launch of several ICBMs.

The probability of an attacking warhead surviving intercepts by three "correlated" layers cannot be known without making assumptions about the mechanisms of the correlation and non-independence of the layers. In general, critics conclude the performance of the system may be no better than the performance of the best layer, and then only if that layer is not saturated by the sheer numbers of missiles, warheads, or countermeasures.

Layered defense proponents are likely to understand, and perhaps agree, with many of these points. But supporters will respond by suggesting these issues can be adequately addressed in the design of a missile defense architecture and adjustments made during its development (see below).

Evolutionary Acquisition Strategy with Spiral Development

Background

The Administration is proposing an acquisition strategy for missile defense that represents a departure from traditional DoD acquisition practices. The proposed approach, called evolutionary acquisition strategy, would not use many of the program milestones and reviews that have long been required for previous major DoD weapon acquisition programs. Evolutionary acquisition is a product of the defense acquisition reform movement and, like other defense acquisition reform initiatives, is aimed at shortening weapon-development times while taking into account the rapidly changing technology environment.[37] Although there appears to be

---

[37] Evolutionary development is an outgrowth of an effort begun by then-Secretary of Defense William Perry in 1994 to streamline DoD's acquisition system, particularly in recognition that future weapon systems would depend in large part on rapidly changing commercial technology. DoD at that time began to shift from a reliance on DoD-unique military specifications to more commercial-oriented performance standards, removed other bureaucratic obstacles to engage the commercial sector, and adopted best business practices, all to align itself more with the way the private

widespread consensus for streamlining the often-cumbersome DoD acquisition system, the Administrations' response to this for missile defense – to employ an evolutionary acquisition strategy – raises potentially significant issues for Congress, particularly regarding program and congressional oversight.

Under an evolutionary acquisition strategy, a basic version of a weapon system is fielded with the intent of subsequently developing and deploying more capable versions of the system as technology and requirements are further refined. A critical aspect of evolutionary acquisition is spiral development, under which the various elements of a weapon system evolve incrementally over time in an iterative manner. Instead of attempting to develop a system that will, upon first deployment, fully satisfy a detailed military requirement, systems under an evolutionary acquisition strategy would be developed, tested, deployed, and modified in a cyclic process that, in principle, would permit weapons developers to incrementally work toward a final system configuration that is eventually capable of meeting its required objectives. Evolutionary acquisition aims to rapidly develop and field useful increments of capability and exploit user feedback in developing additional increments of capability.[38] Weapon life-cycle affordability is an additional stated objective of evolutionary acquisition. DoD has recently developed guidelines for managing weapon-development programs employing evolutionary acquisition.

A distinct characteristic of evolutionary development is a reduced ability, particularly at the outset of a program, to define what the deployed system might look like at various points in the future. Rather than attempting to define final configuration at the outset, evolutionary development consciously treats this issue as an open question to be addressed over time as elements of the system are developed, deployed, evaluated, and modified. In this sense, the Administration's proposed missile defense effort is more of an evolving concept than a typical military system in development.

---

sector operated. A key objective of defense acquisition reform is to reduce the average time needed to develop a complex weapon system – currently more than 11 years – to between 5 and 7 years.

[38] Evolutionary acquisition has been described as a strategy for accommodating constant change throughout the process of developing, deploying and continual operation of a weapon system. A spiral development process might include an iterative set of sub-processes such as: establishing performance objectives, designing, coding/fabricating/integrating, experimenting, testing, assessing operational utility, making tradeoffs, and delivering the system. (Evolutionary Acquisition For C2 Systems. Air Force Instruction 63-123. April 1, 2000. Secretary of the Air Force.)

The Administration's missile defense plan would apply evolutionary acquisition and spiral development to an entire family of system development efforts related to the common mission of missile defense. Under the Administration's plan, missile defense systems would be built, tested, deployed, and evaluated incrementally. The final missile defense system or architecture – that is, the numbers and characteristics of the land-, sea-, air-, and space-based system involved – would be determined gradually over the course of several years. During this period, systems capable of performing similar portions of the missile defense mission (i.e., the boost phase, the midcourse phase, or the terminal phase) would be in implicit competition with one another for places in the final system configuration.

The Administration's plan to employ this acquisition strategy for missile defense is consistent with its view that missile defenses are urgently needed. The Administration argues that deploying missile defenses sooner with less capability than later versions is desirable because any improvement in U.S. missile defense capabilities would complicate enemy planning and thereby strengthen deterrence against ballistic missile attacks. The Administration also argues that the strategy is appropriate for weapon acquisition programs, such as missile defense, where the fundamental technologies involved are less technically mature than they are for well-established types of weapons, such as aircraft and ships.

A major consequence of the Administration's proposed evolutionary acquisition strategy is that the missile-defense program would not feature the well-defined phases and milestones of the traditional DoD acquisition system. Another consequence, already reflected in DoD testimony, is the BMDO cannot provide Congress with a description of its final missile defense architecture, the capabilities of any near- or longer-term system, the specific dates by which most elements of the emerging architecture are to be tested and deployed, an estimate of the eventual total cost of the missile-defense program, or estimates of the amounts of funding that the program will require in individual years beyond FY2002.

Lt. Gen. Ronald Kadish, Director of BMDO (now MDA), stated the following to the Senate in July 2001 in introducing the Administration's missile-defense plan:

> But before I proceed to describe the new program in detail, I would like to make clear what this program does *not* do. It does not define a specific defense. There is no commitment to a procurement program for a full, layered defense. There is no commitment to specific dates for production and deployment other than for lower-tier terminal defense systems....

First, we are recommending a broad, flexible approach to RDT&E that allows us to explore multiple development paths and to reinforce success based on the best technological approaches and the most advantageous basing modes in order to hedge against the inherent uncertainty of the ballistic missile defense challenge. Second, we are recommending an acquisition approach that is evolutionary, one that will allow us to field systems incrementally once they are proven through realistic testing. And third, rather than committing to a single architecture as we have done in the past, we will deploy over time different combinations of sensors and weapons consistent with our national strategic objectives....

This robust RDT&E program aims to demonstrate what does and does not work. Those activities showing the greatest promise will receive greater resource emphasis. Our progress will inform an annual high-level decision-making process that will steer the BMD program in the most promising direction, taking into account optimal approaches and the most reliable information on costs, allowing informed research, production, and deployment decisions....

The business of missile defense requires coping with a number of technological, developmental, acquisition, and threat uncertainties. For this reason, I cannot tell you today what exactly the system will look like 15, 10, or even 5 years from now. This system will take shape over time. We do not intend to lock ourselves into a highly stylized architecture based on either known technologies or hoped for advances in technology that will take a decade or more to complete. We intend to go beyond the conventional build-to-requirements acquisition process....

Specific system choices and time lines will take shape over the next few years through our capability-based, block approach. We will increase our capability over time through an evolutionary process as our technologies mature and are proven through testing. The block approach allows us to put our best, most capable technologies "in play" sooner than would otherwise be possible. We have organized the program with the aim of developing militarily useful capabilities in biannual blocks, starting as early as the 2004-2006 time frame....

We must deviate from the standard acquisition process and recognize the unprecedented technical challenges we are facing. We do not have major [missile] defense acquisition programs in the FY2002 budget. We do not have program activities with traditional fixed milestones and clearly marked phases showing the road to production.

The new approach to BMD development features more streamlined, flexible management through comprehensive and iterative reviews. We will establish yearly decision points to determine the status of the available technologies and concept evaluations in order to be in a position to accelerate, modify, truncate, or terminate efforts in a particular area. This comprehensive annual review process will also help us make decisions to shape the evolving systems and allocate resources to optimally support them.[39]

Issues for Congress

Potential issues for Congress regarding the use of evolutionary acquisition and spiral development in the missile-defense program include the following:

- Evolutionary acquisition with spiral development is a relatively new and untried strategy. Is it the best acquisition strategy for the Administration's high-priority missile defense effort? What are the comparative strengths and weaknesses or evolutionary acquisition and the traditional DoD acquisition system when applied to missile defense? Are there any risks in choosing a large program such as missile defense as one of the first programs to employ this acquisition strategy Compared to a traditional acquisition strategy, what effect would the adoption of an evolutionary acquisition strategy have on time lines for deploying missile defense capabilities, especially in the nearer term? What effect would it have on mitigating the program's technical risks, and on using implicit competition between candidate systems to improve the effectiveness of the overall missile-defense architecture? if there are reasons to not use a traditional acquisition strategy for missile defense, is evolutionary acquisition the only alternative?

- A challenge for DoD, and for the Congress in performing its oversight role, is to reach a workable system of accountability for systems being developed under an evolutionary strategy. What effect might the use of an evolutionary acquisition strategy have on Congress' ability to conduct oversight of missile defense development and procurement? Would such a strategy provide Congress with sufficient opportunities and information to perform its oversight role effectively? From a congressional perspective, what might be the risks of approving the start of a large program for

---

[39] Statement of Lt. Gen. Ronald T. Kadish, USAF, Director, Ballistic Missile Defense Organization, on The Ballistic Missile Defense Program, Amended FY2002 Budget, Before the Senate Armed Services Committee, July 12, 2001, pages 2-3, 6-8, 14. Emphasis as in the original.

which there is no defined final architecture, few specific time lines, and no precise estimates of potential total cost? To what extent, if at all, was the Administration'' choice of an evolutionary acquisition influenced, as some critics contend, by the knowledge that it might relieve the Administration of the responsibility for providing specific answers to congressional questions regarding system architecture, effectiveness, time lines, and cost?[40]

Legislation for FY2002

The Senate Armed Services Committee, in its report (S.Rept. 107-62 of September 12, 2001) on the FY2002 defense authorization bill (S. 1416), stated:

> Despite the large proposed funding increase [for missile defense], the Department of Defense has been extremely vague about its plans for missile defenses. No specific multi-year plan has been proposed. Rather, the Department expects to decide how to proceed with missile defense as it goes along.... These are inadequate justifications for the expenditure of billions of dollars of taxpayer money.... Congress needs to know the general and specific plans for expenditure of missile defense funding, as well as the objectives and projected outyear costs of programs that are begun now. (Page 130)

The committee recommended a provision (section 223) that would require the Secretary of Defense to submit a baseline document for the ballistic missile defense research and development program for the FY2003-FY2007 Future Years Defense Plan (FYDP) submitted to Congress in February 2002 along with the proposed FY2003 defense budget. (See page 13 of the committee's report.)

The conference report (H.Rept. 107-333 of December 12, 2001) on the FY2002 defense authorization bill (S. 1438) included a provision (Section 232) that, among other things, requires the Secretary of Defense to submit to the congressional defense committees, by February 1 each year, a statement of the cost, schedule, testing, and performance goals for DoD's ballistic missile defense programs for the period covered by the FYDP submitted to the Congress that year (Section 232(c)). The Comptroller General, at the end

---

[40] For more on this issue, see, for example, Bradley Graham, Rumsfeld Pares Oversight of Missile Defense Agency, *Washington Post,* February 16, 2002, p. A2.

of FY2002 and FY2003, is to assess the extent to which BMCO (now MDA) has achieved the goals established for the fiscal year in question, and report that assessment to the congressional defense committees by February 15, 2003 and February 15, 2004 (Section 232(g)). The provision also requires the Secretary of Defense to submit to the congressional defense committee an annual program plan, including funding and scheduling data, for "activities planned to be carried out for each missile defense program that enters engineering and manufacturing development" (Section 232(d)). The section also establishes requirements for certain DoD offices to conduct certain annual internal reviews of the program and to report the results of those reviews to the Secretary of Defense and the Director of BMDO (now MDA) (Section 232(e)).

The House Appropriations Committee, in its report (H.Rept. 107-298 of November 19, 2001) on the FY2002 defense appropriations bill (H.R. 3338) stated that the Administration's missile defense plan proposed

> eventually buying and fielding these systems using RDT&E appropriations. The Department's intent is to be able to explore new technologies without an official requirements document and without committing to buy a specific number of systems, as would be required with a major defense acquisition program. This approach is currently used by the Department for technology demonstrations where prototypes are developed in limited quantity as a proof of concept. However, to acquire entire systems under RDT&E would violate fiscal policy, undermine basic program management principles and ignore the distinction between appropriations. Therefore, the committee retains the Department's proposed structure for those technologies that have not yet demonstrated a suitable prototype. However, the Committee directs that funding for a program's EMD [engineering and manufacturing development] activities, and beyond, be budgeted in a separate program element; the program be designated a major defense acquisition program and be subject to the requirements of Milestone II and Milestone III or their equivalents. As the law requires, the actual acquisition of the hardware would be done with procurement funding. (Page 251)

The committee also directed DoD to submit more detailed justification material for the missile defense program as part of its future budget requests, including information on annual missile defense program funding requirements, detailed schedules, test events, and (for missile defense programs that are already major defense acquisition programs) the number of systems to be acquired, the expected performance, the unit cost, and the cost to completion of the program. The committee also directed DoD to "present an overall timeline for its future [missile defense] architecture highlighting when each system in that architecture will go into production as well as a comparable threat timeline indicating which threat systems are expected to be deployed and in what quantities." (Page 252)

The conference report (H.Rept. 107-350 of December 19, 2001) on the FY2002 defense appropriations bill (H.R. 3338) states:

> The conferees support the efforts of the Department [of Defense] to devise a management structure that facilitates integration of the various ballistic missile defense research and development efforts. The Department, however, is cautioned against implementing a management structure and related decision-making process that limit adequate oversight of the program by the Pentagon's operational testing, financial, and programmatic review groups. Also, the conferees will continue to monitor this program's management activities to ensure Congressional oversight. (Page 385)

Ft. Greely Midcourse Alternative

The stated purpose of the Ft. Greely, Alaska, deployment is to provide a realistic test-bed for interceptor missiles linked to the sensor and computer networks of the NMD system. Building and operating a missile silo test-bed in an arctic environment would also be beneficial, according to BMDO. The Administration has stated that the interceptors at Ft. Greely could provide a rudimentary, limited missile defense capability against a rogue-state ICBM in the 2004-2005 period although this contention is disputed. But the principal purpose of the first facilities to be built at Ft. Greely is clearly the testing of the C^3I system and the interoperability of the launcher software with the acquisition, tracking, and targeting systems of an early missile defense system.

Because no live-fire tests from Ft. Greely are contemplated, however, some will argue there is no reason to construct missile launchers today. Rather, the argument goes, the role of the silo launchers could be played equally well by a simple above-ground structure in which the developmental hardware for the launcher (including equipment and software to transfer information to the interceptor) could be installed. Indeed to some this would be a better test bed because the equipment could be reconfigured, replaced, or modified far more rapidly and cheaply than could equipment built into a silo launcher. This has the added benefit of being consistent with the evolutionary acquisition strategy the Administration is pursuing. Given that even the interceptor missile is not itself fully defined, critics will charge it is foolish to build launchers today – when those sunk costs and bored holes might well inhibit any necessary redesign or modification of the final flight hardware. Such a technical compromise, they contend, may also alleviate some ABM Treaty compliance concerns with respect to the Ft. Greely site.

INTERNATIONAL RESPONSE

Russian Hesitancy and Opposition

Even before the Clinton Administration began to focus on a decision on missile defense deployments, Russian officials strongly and consistently objected to U.S. missile defense plans. They argued that the 1972 ABM Treaty remain the "cornerstone of strategic stability," and that missile defenses not permitted by the treaty would not only upset international stability but also undermine Russia's nuclear deterrent.[41] Russian officials also argued that U.S. withdrawal from the ABM Treaty would precipitate Russia's withdrawal from a range of nuclear arms control agreements, including the Intermediate-Range Nuclear Forces (INF) Treaty and the Strategic Arms Reduction Treaties (START I and START II). Russian leaders said they might alto feel compelled to build up their offensive nuclear weapons, or at least deploy multiple warheads on new single-warhead SS-27 missiles, to overcome U.S. missile defenses. Hence, according to the Russian view, U.S. withdrawal from the ABM treaty could precipitate a renewed and broader arms race.

During meetings with the Clinton Administration, Russian officials refused to discuss U.S. proposals for modifications to the ABM Treaty that would have permitted the deployment of a limited, land-based missile defense site in Alaska. Some observers believe that Russia's resistance was due, in part, to Russia's belief that the Clinton Administration was not committed to the deployment of missile defenses and therefore, would not withdraw from the ABM Treaty.

More recently, however, Russia has appeared more willing to consider changing the Treaty. In mid-July 2001, President Putin suggested that the United States and Russia might be able to reach an agreement on missile defenses, as long as the resulting agreement did not upset existing arms

---

[41] For a detailed review of Russia's reaction to U.S. missile defense plans, see *National Missile Defense: Russia's Reaction*. CRS Report RL30967, by Amy F. Woolf.

control regimes.[42] Then, in late July, Presidents Putin and Bush agreed to begin consultations on missile defenses and strategic offensive weapons, with the objective or reaching agreement on a new framework that Administration officials argued might replace the ABM Treaty. After that meeting, Russia's Defense Minister Ivanov stated that he might recommend that Russia accept some changes to the Treaty if the changes would not harm Russia's national security.

Many observers interpreted these changes to indicate that Russia understood that its objections would not stop the Bush Administration's plans to deploy missile defenses or withdraw from the ABM Treaty. Some have argued that president Putin may be willing to accept U.S. proposals to set aside the ABM Treaty and replace it with a new, less formal framework. Others, however, do not believe that Russia has altered its fundamental opposition to U.S. missile defenses and that it continues to support the AMB Treaty. They conclude that, instead of appearing weak by objecting to an inevitable event, President Putin has decided to participate in discussions to bolster his nation's standing as a strategic partner with the United States, to demonstrate to others, especially in Europe, that he is willing to make "responsible compromises," and to try to shape and possibly limit the missile defense system that the United States eventually deploys. This strategy could have advised the apparent Russian willingness, in the weeks before the summit between Presidents Bush and Putin in mid-November, to allow U.S. missile defense tests, as long as the Treaty remained in place to limit defense deployments. Nevertheless, the summit did not produce this type of agreement and the United States informed Russia of its withdrawal from the ABM Treaty on December 13. President Putin referred to the U.S. decision as a mistake, but he, and many of his advisors, noted that this development should not undermine the broader U.S.-relationship. Hence, in spite of earlier warnings of dire consequences, Russia appears resigned to the demise of the ABM Treaty.

Mixed Allied Views in Europe

Most U.S. allies in Europe continue to oppose U.S. withdrawal from the ABM Treaty and the building of a missile defense system, although their

---

[42] Perlez, Jane and Michael Wines. Few Missile Defense Details Emerge After Powell Talks. *New York Times*, July 19, 2001.

opposition softened and became more nuanced since Spring 2001. They do not find persuasive that the attack of September 11, 2001, strengthens the argument for missile defense. In general, the allies support a continued treaty regime between the United States and Russia that provides structure to the strategic weapons balance. A U.S.-Russian agreement to reduce nuclear forces has been greeted with relief in Europe, but most allies are quietly critical of the U.S. decision to abandon the ABM Treaty, which they view as an act of "unilateralism."

In general, most U.S. allies in Europe have argued that robust missile defenses, if coupled with unilateral abrogation of the ABM Treaty, would likely upset stability, ignite arms races, and undermine international non-proliferation objectives. They tend to view the Administration's effort to move forward with missile defense as too narrow an effort to confront the problem of proliferation of weapons of mass destruction and their means of delivery. In their view, a broader effort is necessary; for example, they believe that the United State should not have refused to sign the Biological Weapons Protocol.

Many European governments voided their views on missile defense during President Bush's trip to Europe in June 2001. although grateful that the Administration agreed to consult with them over missile defense, many European officials complained that the meetings were vague on details for Administration plans and that their views were not taken into account. However, some governments have endorsed the Administration's missile defense plans, such as Italy and Spain. The responses of France, Germany, and Britain ranged from critical to reserved. while each of these governments acknowledges a growing ballistic missile threat from "rogue states," particularly Iraq, they do not believe that missile defense can provide necessary security.

France is the most forceful EU critic of missile defense. President Jacques Chirac calls the ABM Treaty the "strategic pillar" of arms control; in his view, its abrogation will undermine nuclear deterrence and impel countries to build weapon systems able to penetrate a missile defense system. France, a nuclear power, believes that deterrence remains effective against countries such as Russia as well as Iraq. German Chancellor Gerhard Schroeder also acknowledges potential missile threats from such countries as Iraq, but believes that economic and diplomatic engagement can counter such threats. Germany is one of several EU countries, for example, seeking expanded trade relations and political contact with Iran. British officials are generally more agnostic on missile defense, but the Labor government of Prime Minister Tony Blair presented the Bush Administration with a report signed by approximately 250 Labor Members in the House of Commons in July 2001 that was critical of missile defense. Prime Minister Blair has said that Mr. Bush is right to raise missile defense as part of "new and imaginative solutions" to the proliferation of weapons of mass destruction, but has also called for a structured approach through arms control agreements to achieve this end.[43]

The Europeans remain quietly critical of the Administration's missile defense program and the decision to abrogate the ABM Treaty. However, U.S. cooperation with Russia in Afghanistan, combined with NATO's decision in late February 2002 to establish a more substantial joint council with Russia, have softened concern among the allies that the Administration was ignoring or marginalizing Moscow. At the same time, the Administration's reluctance to use treaties to manage arms control has sustained a European belief that the United States will push aside potential international agreements that might limit Washington's arms policies.

Diverse Reaction in Asia and the Pacific

The Administration's missile defense policy has received a very mixed reception among the countries of the Asia-Pacific region. Reaction has ranged from harsh criticism from China through expressions of anxiety in Southeast Asia, "understanding" in Japan, and support from Australia and India.

Chinese Opposition

The People's Republic of China (PRC) opposes U.S. missile defense efforts strongly and vociferously. The PRC's objections are at least three-fold: First, Chinese civilian and military leaders are concerned that the possession by the United States of an ICBM defense capability would seriously degrade the effectiveness – and hence the deterrent value – of

---

[43] Interviews with officials of EU governments, summer 2001; "Les antimissiles deviennent l'enjeu d'un nouveau défi euro-atlantique," *Le Monde*, June 21, 2001, p. 17; "Bush tries to sell NATO on Missile Defense plan," *Washington Post*, June 14, 2001, p. A1; "'Star Wars' fears may test US-UK relations," *Financial Times*, July 11, 2001, p. 12. Some of these concerns echo European concerns of the 1980s. See *The Strategic Defense Initiative and U.S. Alliance Strategy*, Archived CRS Report 85-48, by Paul Gallis, Mark Lowenthal, and Marcia Smith, Feb. 1, 1985.

China's 20-25 CSS-4 liquid fueled ICBMs, their only missiles with sufficient range to reach the continental United States.[44] Although the Bush Administration has emphasized that its long-range missile defense effort is designed primarily to deal with small-scale attacks by "rogue" nations, Chinese policymakers assume that a protective shield against these nations in all probability would include enough interceptor missiles to threaten the viability of its own force.

Second, the simultaneous pursuit by the United States of missile defenses against short- and theater-range ballistic missiles would allow U.S. forces in the Pacific to deploy a protective shield over Taiwan, thereby potentially negating China's ability to gain the upper hand in a cross-Strait confrontation with what it regards as a renegade province. China also appears concerned that the United States might transfer BMD technology to Taiwan.

Third, Beijing is concerned about U.S.-Japanese missile defense cooperation. Despite the fact that Japan possesses only a very limited offensive military capability, Beijing's strategists and many outside analysts regard Japan's forces as more technologically advanced and more operationally effective. China's frequently expressed concerns about a revival of Japanese militarism are in part political weapons in a struggle for regional influence, but they also reflect a strong, historical and emotionally-rooted wariness of Japanese intentions. Thus China remains highly suspicious of any developments that appear to make the U.S.-Japan security alliance more effective or that give Japan additional military capabilities.

American and foreign critics of the Bush Administration's missile defense effort cite the likelihood that China will respond to a U.S. missile defense capability by building more missiles with more sophisticated warheads – for instance by deploying multiple independent reentry vehicles (MIRVs) that would present more difficult targeting challenges. Supporters of the Administration's policy argue that, whatever the United States does, China already has plans to increase the size and sophistication of its ICBM force.

Noncommittal Japanese "Understanding"

Although the Japanese government and public are deeply troubled by the Bush Administration's approach to missile defense, Tokyo has withheld criticism, employing the time-honored Japanese expression of

---

[44] For further information on China's missile capabilities, see CRS Report 97-391, *China: Ballistic and Cruise Missiles*, by Shirley A. Kan.

"understanding" U.S. policy.[45] Japan's cooperation would be essential if the United States were to seek to develop an integrated regional missile defense architecture. Even an independent Japanese missile defense capability against short- and theater-range missiles, if it were interoperable with that of the United States, could enhance the ability of U.S. forces to mount a regional anti-missile defense. Unconstrained use of several current U.S. bases in Japan would also become important if the United States were to deploy a boost-phase missile defense capability to counter long-range missiles from North Korea – a prime concern of U.S. missile defense advocates.

Japan had engaged in discussion with the United States about cooperating on missile defense since the early mid-1980s, but had resisted committing itself until North Korea's August 1998 launch of a three-stage Taep'o-dong 1 medium-range missile, which passed over the main Japanese island of Honshu. In August 1999, U.S. and Japanese officials agreed to carry out joint research on elements of the Navy Theater-Wide (NTW) program (now known as the Sea-Based Boost program), an exo-atmospheric system that might be deployed on ships fielding the Aegis radar and fire control system. (Japan already has four of these destroyers, and has budgeted for two more.)

Japanese defense policymakers and defense firms generally have been enthusiastic about non-strategic missile defense cooperation (i.e., missile defense designed to counter short- and theater-range ballistic missiles), but the political parties and the public are split over the issue. Many Japanese defense officials and observers see such cooperation as a counter to North Korea's missiles and an "alliance builder" with the United States. Other Japanese are fearful of aggravating relations with China or triggering an Asian missile race – concerns that are shared by many U.S. critics. Even missile defense advocates are concerned about the large costs associated with the proposed Sea-Based Midcourse effort. Moreover, if, as expected, this particular program leads to an expanded role in seeking to provide missile defenses against long-range missiles, then support in Japan is likely to erode quickly.

Japanese officials have indicated two serious concerns about the Bush Administration's decision to treat NMD and TMD programs as

---

[45] For additional background and analysis concerning Japanese policy see CRS Report RL30992, *Japan-U.S. Cooperation on Theater Missile Defense*, by Richard P. Cronin and Y. Jane Nokano.

undifferentiated aspects of missile defense. First, the use of Japanese-supplied technology in the U.S. effort aimed at engaging ICBMs would violate a constitutional ban on "collective defense." Second, the new U.S. approach may concentrate resources on technologies that are less relevant to Japan's particular missile defense concerns. Japan is concerned only with the threat posed by theater-range missiles, whereas the Bush Administration has given first priority to achieving a near-term capability against long-range threats to the United States. In addition, Japan, like the countries of Southeast Asia, is concerned about the effect of the new missile defense policy on further polarizing Sino-U.S. relations, making Sino-Japanese relations more difficult.

For the time being, Japanese officials have avoided addressing the collective defense issue arising out of the changed U.S. missile defense strategy and have concentrated on protecting Japan's option to acquire a BMD capability. Towards that end, Japan has boosted its budget for BMD cooperation and signaled its intent to acquire the technology that could support a BMD capability on the two new Aegis destroyers that are under construction.[46] With regard to funding, Japan initially budgeted about $30-35 million annually for a five-year period for research and development cooperation on the NTW program. In late August 2001, however, the JDA announced its intent to seek twice as much – $66.5 million at prevailing exchange rates – for the next fiscal year, which begins April 1, 2002. This increase is being sought despite severe overall pressures on the defense budget, which reportedly will only increase by 1.8% overall in fiscal year 2001.[47] For its part, the Department of Defense has included comparable funding in its future year defense plans.

Australian Support

The conservative government of Prime Minister John Howard has given cautiously phrased support to the Bush Administration's missile defense policy and more generally has welcomed the emphasis placed by the Administration on strengthening U.S. relations with Asia-Pacific allies. Canberra's support appears primarily a matter of promoting closer alliance relations, but it also stems from the desire to benefit from enhancements to the U.S. defense "umbrella." Among other concerns, Australian officials note that their territory is within range of North Korea's Taep'o-dong 2

---

[46] *Tokyo Shimbun*, August 17, 2001: 1.
[47] *Nihon Keizai Shimbun* report cited in *Japan Digest*, August 30. 2001: 4-5.

missile, were it to be successfully developed and deployed. Australia has qualified its support for the new U.S. missile defense strategy by noting its preference that the issue of the ABM treaty be resolved between the United States and Russia by consensus, and not by a unilateral American abandonment of the treaty. Public attitudes are mixed. The Labor Party is divided between those who oppose any participation in the U.S. missile defense effort, and those who only oppose research and development cooperation.

A major issue in Australia is the question of what role the Pine Gap relay ground station, jointly operated by U.S. and Australian forces, would play in U.S. NMD. (Pine Gap has the capability of capturing and relaying satellite data on missile launches in the East Asian region.) For reasons that are unclear, the latest Australian defense white paper reportedly makes no reference to ballistic missile defense, though it does discuss a growing threat to its naval forces from supersonic anti-ship missiles. Apart from the opposition to missile defense of the Labor Party, Australian policy over the longer run could be affected by several concerns. In the past, Australia has been uncomfortable when the United States emphasized alliance relations over multilateral for a such as the ASEAN Regional Forum, because from the Australian perspective such for a make its alliance cooperation with the United States more acceptable to Asian neighbors.

Uncharacteristic Indian Support

In a notable break with its traditional opposition to U.S. nuclear and missile policy initiatives, the Indian coalition government led by the Hindu-nationalist Bharatiya Janata Party (BJP) reacted warmly to the Bush Administration's missile defense policy. Indian leaders were pleased at being included in a May 2001 briefing tour of Asian capitals by Deputy Secretary of State Richard L. Armitage, which also included Tokyo and Seoul. India's response, inconceivable until very recently, appears to be based on a number of considerations. First, the Bush Administration appears willing, at least symbolically, to give India recognition that it has long sought – tacit admission to the "nuclear club" of the big powers. Second, and more concretely, the Administration has signaled its desire to seek congressional approval to relieve India of remaining sanctions that were imposed following its series of nuclear tests in May 1998; these include a ban on military sales and the transfer of controlled technology. Third, the Administration appears to have informally granted India long-sought recognition as the premier powers in South Asia, and the status of a putative security partner. Fourth, India has a natural interest in any technology that could counter China's ballistic missiles, and may hope to one day obtain a missile defense capability with U.S. assistance. Last, but not least, the Administration's proposal to substantially reduce U.S. missile inventories fits in with India's long-standing insistence that it will not sign the Comprehensive Test Ban Treaty (CTBT) or participate in other anti-nuclear agreements until the major weapons powers substantially reduce their own arsenals. This gesture by the Administration has given the Indian Government some defense against criticism that it has completely reversed a policy of nearly three decades.

The Bush Administration's policy appears to recognize frankly that India's nuclear and missile capability is a reality, and seeks to engage constructively with a friendly democracy of significant military power and geostrategic weight. Whether or not a *quid pro quo* for Indian support of its missile defense policy, the desire of the Bush Administration to remove the remaining anti-nuclear sanctions represents a significant reversal of basic American nuclear non-proliferation policy dating from the mid-1970s. Although the Clinton Administration and the 106th Congress had moved swiftly to waive most non-military sanctions against both India and Pakistan following their May 1998 nuclear tests, these legislative initiatives were rationalized on humanitarian grounds or out of consideration for American farmers and businesses. A number of critics of U.S. nuclear nonproliferation policy, however, have long called for "realism" about the inevitability that India will become a nuclear weapons power with strategic reach (and that Pakistan will become a regional nuclear power). In this sense, the policy initiative could be viewed as the triumph of this point of view.

Some also see engagement with India as part of a *de facto* policy of seeking to counterbalance China's rising power by bolstering security ties with regional allies and other friendly states. Senior Administration officials insist that the new security initiative is not directed at China, but is related to shared U.S. and Indian values of democratic government and the common experience of multi-ethnicity.[48] Critics note that the Indian polity has long possessed these characteristics – a fact that did not heretofore reduce U.S. opposition to New Delhi's nuclear and missile programs. Hence, the Administration may be challenged by critics in Congress and elsewhere to further explain the basis for its policy change towards India.

---

[48] Department of State, International Information programs, *Transcript Excerpts: Armitage on Mideast, South Asia*. Washington File, Aug. 17, 2001 (Excerpts from August 17 Sydney Media Roundtable).

BACKGROUND ON MAJOR MISSILE DEFENSE PROGRAMS

Boost Defense Segment

Air-Based Boost

The Air-Based Boost program, more commonly known as the Airborne Laser (ABL), would use a high-power chemical laser mounted in a modified Boeing 747 aircraft to shoot down theater missiles in their powered boost phase of flight. The laser would seek to rupture or damage the missile's booster skin to cause the missile to lose thrust or flight control and fall short of the intended target before decoys, warheads, or submunitions are deployed. The ABL's intended range is several hundred kilometers. Major subsystems include the lethal laser, a high-precision tracking system for keeping the laser beam on target, and an adaptive optics system that compensates for atmospheric effects to keep the beam tightly focused.

The ABL program was transferred to BMDO, now the MDA, from the Air Force. The MDA states there is no current system or architecture envisioned for missile defense, including specifics for the ABL. But the Director of BMDO, in congressional testimony, has stated that "BMDO will evaluate the most promising projects" for boost-phase defense "to provide a basis for an architecture decision between 2003 and 2005."

The most recent Air Force concept envisioned a fleet of seven aircraft. Five of these aircraft would deploy to a theater to support two 24-hour combat air patrols. These aircraft would be positioned behind the friendly line of troops and moved closer toward enemy airspace as local air superiority is achieved. The most recent cost estimate was $10.7 billion (life cycle costs), which includes an estimated $1.6 billion for the current program development and risk reduction phase.

Funding for FY2001 was $387 million, including a supplemental appropriation of $153 million approved in July 2001. Both the House and Senate armed services committees and the Senate Appropriations Committee increased funding for the ABL above the original FY2001 request.

BMDO requested $410 million for the ABL in FY2002 to support an increased level of near-term testing and technology development. Although the House and Senate authorization reports each recommended reduced funding, the final FY2002 appropriation increased ABL funding to $484 million because the program had been slipping and many in Congress wanted the ABL to get back on schedule. Although details are not yet available, one report suggests that the MDA will request $598 million for the ABL in the FY2003 budget.

The contractor team consists of Boeing, Lockheed Martin, and TRW. Boeing is responsible for the aircraft and for overall management, including systems integration. Lockheed Martin is responsible for the beam control systems, including target tracking and atmospheric compensation. TRW is responsible for the lethal laser and for ground support systems. There are numerous subcontractors.

The system currently under development will attempt its first missile shoot-down test in 2003. BMDO states this half-power ABL could be available for deployment as an emergency capability immediately following lethality demonstrations scheduled for late 2003. If all goes according to schedule, this system and the next two could provide an initial operating capability – one aircraft on station, on preparing to arrive on station, and one on ground alert – by FY2009.

Congressional concerns about the ABL have centered on two main issues: the maturity of key technologies and the concept of operations. First, although proponents contend that the ABL employs mature technology, others characterize key aspects (particularly the atmospheric compensation system) as experimental. Critics also claim that the tests needed to resolve this question, which are being conducted concurrently with the development of the technology, will not take place until 2003. This date is after a second aircraft is scheduled to be ordered, and just months before the first shoot-down test. The compressed and concurrent nature of this schedule also is an issue of concern. The Defense Department's Office of Test and Evaluation informed Congress in its FY2000 annual report (January 2001) that the 24-month EMD (Engineering, Manufacturing, and Development) program is "alarmingly short….[the schedule] allows for no technical problems or test failures, and the many integration and test activities cannot all physically be accomplished in the time allotted for EMD."

Second, there is disagreement about whether the ABL would be operationally effective, even it its technology performs as planned. The ability of the ABL to destroy enemy missiles at its intended range depends on a number of factors, including atmospheric conditions between the laser and the target, possible enemy countermeasures, and the worldwide trend towards deployment of longer-range missiles for theater operations. Possible technical countermeasures include hardening the missile casing, spinning the missile, or applying a polished finish to the missile.

In addition, the ability to deploy ABL aircraft during crisis or war will depend on the ability to provide a relatively safe area of operations through air superiority. It is not clear whether enemy forces would wait for this to happen and render their ballistic missile forces more vulnerable, or see incentives to launch their missiles before ABL systems were deployed, or whether an opponent might choose to wait out a crisis because a force of ABL aircraft probably would not be deployed on 24-hour combat patrols indefinitely.

Space-Based Boost

The mission of the Space-Based Boost intercept portion of the program is to develop the capability of shooting down ballistic missiles of any range in their boost phase (i.e., before the missiles have released their payload) from platforms located in orbit. The primary effort is focused on developing a space-based laser (SBL), the components of which have been under development since before SDI in the early 1980s. In addition, research and developing in space-based kinetic weapons is to be reconstituted. Other missions for the SBL in the past have included surveillance, target detection and designation, and air defense.

The FY2002 amended budget request for this element of the program is $190 million; SBL activities account for $170 million. The other $20 million requested would go toward study and definition of potential kinetic energy boost phase interceptor concepts and a space-based kinetic energy experiment (SBX) to demonstrate them.

The primary objective of the SBL activity is to be able to conduct a SBL Integrated Flight Experiment (an in-orbit demonstration) in the 2011-2013 time frame. Activities include risk-reduction development of component subsystems (a megawatt hydrogen-fluoride laser, mirrors, beam controls, pointing/tracking/fire controls, etc.), component integration, ground testing, launch integration and on-orbit testing. Funding also would go toward the construction of a new SBL Test Facility (which is to be built at the Stennis Space Flight Center in Mississippi). The Administration has not released a total life-cycle cost required to achieve this goal. In the past, estimates have suggested that the test could be accomplished with a 5 to 6 year program costing between $1 billion and $3 billion. Those estimates are generally seen as overly optimistic today. Note, too, that this just covers the demonstration experiment. The design, development, testing, launch, and operation of a constellation of a dozen or more SBL satellites would require additional funding.

The contract team working on the SBL include divisions of TRW, Boeing, and Lockheed Martin located in California.

There are a number of issues associated with space-based boost phase intercept. Perhaps the primary one is that testing and deploying these systems in an ABM mode has been prohibited by the ABM Treaty. Any such system could also function as a anti-satellite weapon, which issue has also been highly controversial. The desirability of stationing weapons in space generates differing opinions. Also, the technical hurdles associated with space-based interceptors – especially lasers, with their weight, size, and reliability constraints – are difficult. Feasibility is not yet certain, hence the need for the demonstration programs. At the very least, how long it will take to overcome those hurdles and at what cost remains uncertain.

Congress was not supportive of the space-based intercept portion of the boost phase segment of the program. The House, in considering the defense authorization bill, voted to cut $120 million from the space-based intercept program. Rep. Spratt argued later that the cut was made because most Members wanted to see if the laser technology could prove itself first on an airborne platform before trying to put that technology on a space-based platform. This reduction was restored in conference. Nevertheless, in the end, Congress did not support the space-based intercept program in the defense appropriations bill. Congress voted to reduce the request for the space-based laser by $140 million ($120 million for the program and another $20 million for a space-based boost study), leaving $30 million to continue the program. The space-based kinetic intercept program was cut by $10 million (specifically for a study), leaving $10 million for that program. In all, $40 million was appropriated for the Space-Based Boost program.

The large cut in the space-based laser program, unless somehow reversed, is likely to cause a major restructuring, if not cancellation, of the work on the SBL Integrated Flight Experiment. The cut also threatens to halt construction of the SBL Test Facility.

Sea-Based Boost

The Sea-Based Boost program was created by the Bush Administration in 2001 as part of its new missile defense program. (The general idea of using sea-based missiles to intercept enemy ballistic missiles in their boost-phase, however, goes back several years.) The Administration's $685 million FY2002 request for all Boost Defense Segment programs included $50 million for the program, which amount Congress approved in its final defense appropriations bill. The FY2003 Boost Defense Segment request is about $800 million; at this time the specific request for sea-based boost is not publicly available, but is likely to be comparable to last year's request.

The sea-based boost program is not yet well defined. MDA Director Kadish stated in July 2001 that the project "is considering a high-speed, high-acceleration booster coupled with a boost kill vehicle. This same booster will be evaluated (with a different kill vehicle) for sea-based midcourse roles."[49] The program could be pursued as either a complement to air-and space-based boost-defense systems or a hedge against the possibility of technical problems in these other programs. General Kadish stated the BMDO is "going to institute concept studies and [is] looking at concepts on how to do the boost phase with kinetic energy, as a hedge against the directed energy, should be run into problems there. So we have some experiments in space with the space-based laser, and we're looking at whether we should be doing some experiments in space with kinetic energy that build on the terrestrial side for airborne laser and a sea-based kinetic energy killer."[50]

One press report stated that

> The approach [for Sea-Based Boost] differs greatly, however, from the boost-phase intercept concepts [previously] considered by the Navy. The service was eyeing its traditional Standard Missile interceptor as the baseline for any attempts to shoot down ballistic missiles during their first seconds of flight. The BMDO concept, however, is an entirely different missile.[51]

The sea-based boost-defense concept is of potential interest because forward-deployed Navy ships operating off the coasts of other countries might be close enough to certain ballistic missile launch sites of concern for high-speed, high-acceleration, ship-launched interceptors to fly inland from the ship and intercept enemy ballistic missiles during the boost phase. The interceptor would need a kill vehicle different from the Sea-based Midcourse

---

[49] Statement of Lieutenant General Ronald T. Kadish, USAF, Director, Ballistic Missile Defense Organization, on The Ballistic Missile Defense Program, Amended Fiscal Year 2002 Budget, Before the Senate Armed Services Committee, July 12, 2001, page 26.
[50] Transcript of July 13, 2001 DoD news briefing on missile defense with Lt. Gen. Kadish.
[51] Wall, Robert, Pentagon Embraces Murky Missile Defenses. *Aviation Week & Space Technology*, July 23, 2001: 27.

kill vehicle because the latter is designed to operate against a small and relatively cold target, while a boost-defense kill vehicle would need to be capable of operating against a large and hot-burning target. The sea-based boost-defense concept appears most feasible for use against missiles launched from sites that are close or somewhat close to international waters, since this would reduce the distance that the interceptor would need to fly to reach the enemy missile and thereby increase the chance that the interceptor would reach it during its boost phase. The concept might thus have the most potential for intercepting missiles launched from countries such as North Korea, Libya, or perhaps Iran. The concept would appear to offer little potential for intercepting long-range Russian or Chinese missiles, whose launch sites are located deep inland, because these missiles are more likely to complete their boost phase before a ship-launched interceptor (even one with a high-speed, high-acceleration booster) could reach them.

Legislation for FY2002

In its report (H.Rept. 107-194 of September 4, 2001) on the FY2002 defense authorization bill (H.R. 2586), the House Armed Services Committee recommended reducing the funding request for Sea-Based Boost by $25 million, "reflecting the committee's view that concept definition and operational assessment should precede hardware design, development, and testing." (Page 235.)

In its report (S.Rept. 107-62 of September 12, 2001) on the FY2002 defense authorization bill (S. 1416), the Senate Armed Services committee recommended reducing the funding for the concept-definition portion of the request for Sea-Based Boost by $10 million. The committee states that it "understands that the design of the new booster does not yet exist, and that the Navy has not been involved in the conceptual design process. Boost-phase technology is extremely challenging, and since boost-phase hardware does not yet exist, it is unlikely that actual tests of such hardware would be warranted or possible in the first year of such an initiative." The committee urged BMDO (now MDA) "to involve the Navy in sea-based boost concept development before proceeding further." (Page 213)

Midcourse Defense Segment

Ground-Based Midcourse

The Ground-based Midcourse Program, also known previously as the National Missile Defense (NMD) program, would use some number of ground-based interceptors to seek to defend all 50 states of the United States from a limited intercontinental-range ballistic missile attack. The kinetic kill warhead on the missile would seek to destroy its intended target through direct collision during the midcourse phase of the attacking missile or warhead. Major subsystems might include some number of existing and new radars and surveillance platforms, including the Aegis Spy-1 radar, existing early warning radars and a new X-Band radar, the space-based Defense Support Program, SBIRS (High and Low), and various Battle Management, Command, Control, and Communications (BMC^3) components.

The Ground-Based Midcourse program is BMDO's proposed successor to the National Missile Defense (NMD) program. The Administration has not proposed a system at this juncture, but it has indicated the Midcourse Test Bed, in conjunction with the 5 proposed interceptor missiles to be deployed at Ft. Greely, could provide a rudimentary ground-based ICBM defense contingency capability beginning about 2004-2005. Some have suggested an additional capability a few years after this with about 50 missiles and the new X-Band radar. Boeing is the Lead System Integrator (LSI).

For point of reference, the Clinton Administration considered deploying a system of 100 ground-based interceptors in Alaska at a cost of about $36 billion (the life-cycle cost was estimated to be about $44.5 billion through FY2026). The Initial Operational Capability (IOC) for this system was 2005.

The Bush Administration requested $3.23 billion for the Ground-Based Midcourse program in FY2002, which Congress approved. Congress approved about $2 billion for FY2001. In Congress, both House and Senate armed services committees added funds to the Clinton Administration's FY2001 NMD request for risk reduction measures in the program, and the Senate Appropriations Committee added some money for risk reduction and additional radar development.

The NMD program has witnesses a number of technical challenges. These include ongoing delays in testing the rocket booster, which in turn has adversely affected decisions on acquiring long-lead interceptor technologies. In addition, modeling and simulation tools that were supposed to aid the Clinton Administration in its decision whether to deploy a limited NMD in

Alaska, were delivered too late to help in that decision. The Integrated Flight Test (IFT) program also has achieved uncertain results. Although many tests were called successful by the DoD, post-intercept test analyses have been considered more ambiguous. Much of this debate centers over the degree to which target missiles or warheads were artificially enhanced to make the intercept more likely. Program delays have occurred regularly. But, a great number of IFT objectives were designed to test other aspects of the missile launch, missile flight, and interceptor performance. These other, non-intercept objectives were largely considered successful.

In early December 2001, BMDO announced a successful NMD intercept test over the central Pacific Ocean. MBDO stated this test is a major step in an "aggressive test program," and that it was the "third successful intercept test in five attempts."

Sea-Based Midcourse

The Sea-Based Midcourse program is the successor to the Navy Theater-Wide (NTW) program (which was also called the Navy Upper Tier program). The Administration's $3,200 million FY2003 request for Midcourse Defense Segment programs includes an amount not yet publicly available for the Sea-Based Midcourse program. Major contractors for the program are Boeing of Seattle, Washington, Lockheed Martin of Moorestown, New Jersey and Sunnyvale, California, Raytheon of Tucson, Arizona, and Thiokol of Promontory, Utah.

The Navy's NTW program was originally designed to intercept theater ballistic missiles during the midcourse phase of flight, so as to provide theater-wide (i.e., regional) defense of U.S. and friendly forces, vital military and political assets ashore, and large geographic areas. The system would be based on navy Aegis ships.[52] It would involve modifying the Aegis ships' radars to improve their ability to detect and track ballistic missiles, and developing a new version of the Standard Missile known as the SM-3. Compared to the earlier SM-2 missile, the SM-3 would incorporate a third-stage rocket motor to give the missile a higher speed (i.e., a higher "burn-out velocity"), and a kinetic kill vehicle (KKV) called the Lightweight Exo-

---

[52] Aegis ships are cruisers and destroyers equipped with the Aegis air defense system, the Navy's most capable surface-ship air-defense system. The Aegis system is a highly integrated combination of sensors (including the SPY-1 phased array radar, which is unique to Aegis ships), computers, software, displays, weapon launchers and weapons. The Navy's Aegis ships are the Ticonderoga (CG-47) class cruisers and Arleigh Burke (DDG-51) class destroyers.

Atmospheric Projectile (LEAP) that destroys the enemy missile by colliding with it.

BMDO Director Kadish's July 12, 2001 testimony suggests that the Administration's plan for Sea-Based Midcourse is to proceed with development of the capability envisaged under the NTW program, deploy it, and work toward improving the system so that it can eventually be used against longer-range missiles:

> The Sea-Based Midcourse System is intended to intercept hostile missiles in the ascent phase of midcourse flight, which when accompanied by [the] ground-based system, provides a complete midcourse layer [of defense].... The Sea-Based Midcourse System will build upon technologies in the existing Aegis Weapon System and the Standard Missile infrastructures and will be used against short and medium-range threats. Funding in FY2002 offers the ability to continue testing and enables a potential contingency sea-based midcourse capability that can grant limited defense to U.S. and allied deployed forces as an element of the BMD System Block 2004. To support this effort five flight tests of the sea-based midcourse system are planned in FY2002. Funding also begins concept development and risk reduction work for advanced capability blocks to include more robust capability against intermediate and long-range threats to complement Ground-Based Midcourse capabilities later this decade.[53]

When asked at a news briefing about when the Sea-Based Midcourse would become a working part of the BMD system, Kadish stated:

> there are two answers to that question. It could be relatively close, in the next five years, if you will, against short- and medium-range missiles, based on the results of the Aegis LEAP interceptor tests that are about to begin this September. Okay? Those [NTW components] were designed [for use] against shorter-range missiles.
> [Providing sea-based midcourse defense against] longer-range missiles is going to take more time, and we're going to aggressively pursue the complementary nature of that. And if we can find a very realistic approach to doing that more rapidly we will, but my expectation right now is that it will be the end of the decade before we can actually get those [improved sea-based midcourse] systems potentially into an [overall BMD]

---

[53] Statement of Lieutenant General Ronald T. Kadish, USAG, Director, Ballistic Missile Defense Organization, on The Ballistic Missile Defense Program, Amended Fiscal Year 2002 Budget, Before the Senate Armed Services Committee, July 12, 2001, page 24.

architecture, and maybe in the '07 and '08 time frame for tests. We'll just have to wait and see based on the results of this.

General Kadish also stated that "the sea-based tests start in September [2001], we have another one in December [2002], and then about one every other month after that, as I recall, depending on how successful they are.[54] The program is now in the middle of a series of nine test flights.

Improving the NTW system so that it can be used against longer-range missiles could involve making further modifications to the Aegis ships' radars. It would almost certainly involve developing a larger and higher-speed missile than the SM-3, which has a maximum speed (i.e., burn-out velocity) of between 3.0 and 3.5 kilometers per second (kps). The Navy reportedly has been considering 3 different options for a higher-speed missile:[55]

- **Faster SM-3.** This missile, also referred to as the SM-3 Block 1 or the Enhanced NTW missile, would extend the 21-inch diameter of the SM-3's first-stage booster up through the second stage, but retain the Standard Missile's original 13.5-inch diameter above that point. It would have a range of 1,000 kilometers and a maximum speed of 4.5 kps, and it would carry an improved version of the NTW missile's LEAP KKV weighing about 30 kilograms.

- **Enhanced SM-3.** This missile, also referred to as the SM-3 Block 2 or the Improved 8-Pack missile, would increase the diameter of the Standard Missile along its entire length to 21 inches – the maximum diameter than can be fired from the Mk 41 vertical launch system (VLS) installed on Aegis ships. (The Mk 41 VLS is installed on Navy ships in modules that each contain 8 missile-launch tubes, leading to the use of the term 8-pack.) This missile would have a range of 1,500 kilometers and a maximum speed of 5.5 kps, and it would carry a more capable KKV weighing about 40 kilograms.

---

[54] Transcript of July 13, 2001 DoD news briefing on missile defense with Lt. Gen. Kadish.
[55] Sources for information on missile options: Ratnam, Gopal. U.S. Navy To Play Larger Role In Missile Defense. *Defense News*, January 21-27, 2002; 10; Holzer, Robert. U.S. Navy Seeks Larger Share of Antimissile Funds. *Defense News,* April 9, 2001: 1, 44 (graphic on page 1); Sirak, Michael C. White House Decision May Move Sea-Based NMD Into Spotlight. *Inside Missile Defense*, September 6, 2000: 1; Holzer, Robert. DoD Weighs Navy Interceptor Options. *Defense News*, July 24, 2000: 1, 60 (graphic on page 1); Holzer, Robert. U.S. Navy Gathers Strength, Allies in NMD Showdown. *Defense News*, March 15, 1999: 1, 42 (graphic on page 1).

- **New Missile.** This missile, also referred to as the Standard Missile 27 or the 6-Pack missile, would have a diameter of 27 inches and a longer length than the Standard Missile, and would be fired from a new VLS designed to accommodate missiles of that diameter and length. This new VLS could have 6 missile-launch-tube modules occupying the same deck area as the 8-tube modules of the current Mk 41 VLS, leading to the use of the term 6-pack. This missile would have a range of more than 1,500 kilometers and a maximum speed of 6.5 kps, and it would carry an even more capable KKV – wither the same KKV being developed for the land-based NMD system or an advanced-technology KKV – weighing about 50 kilograms.

On January 25, 2002, a test flight of the NTW system achieved an apparently successful hit-to-kill against an Aries theater ballistic missile target using its LEAP KKV. This flight was the fourth in the planned series of nine test flights.[56]

In addition to the Aegis-ship program described above, the Administration has also stated that it will explore the concept of placing an X-band missile tracking and engagement radar (perhaps like the one planned for Alaska) on one or more ships as complements or substitutes for land-based X-band radars. The United States over the years has outfitted and operated several merchant-type ships with similar radars to support flight tests of U.S. ballistic missiles and reportedly to learn about the characteristics of foreign ballistic missiles.

Legislation for FY2002

In its report (H.Rept. 107-194 of September 4, 2001) on the FY2002 defense authorization bill (H.R. 2586), the House Armed Services Committee recommended reducing the funding request for the concept definition studies potion of Sea-Based Midcourse by $30 million, stating that "The committee believes that ongoing, competitive radar development activities will greatly influence the course this effort will take." (Page 235)

In its report (S.Rept. 107-62 of September 12, 2001), on the FY2002 defense authorization bill (S. 1416), the Senate Armed Services committee

---

[56] Wall, Robert. Intercept Starts Long Road To Sea-Based Missile Defense. *Aviation Week & Space Technology*, February 4, 2002; Interceptor Hits Target In Navy Anti-Missile Test. *Washington Post*, January 26, 2002: 5; Sea-Based Midcourse Test Completed. Department of Defense News Release No. 037-02, January 26, 2002.

commented extensively on the Sea-Based Midcourse program and recommended reducing funding for various portions of the program. With regard to funding for procurement of interceptor missiles, the committee stated:

> The proposed interceptor procurement would start prior to the completion of the ambitious series of intercept tests of the system, planned for fiscal year 2002. Moreover, problems with the Navy Theater-Wide interceptor divert system, which is critical to the interceptor's ability to hit a target, call into question the reliability and affordability of the interceptor design. Therefore, the committee believes it would be unwise to procure extra interceptors at this time, and recommends a reduction of $100.0 million for that purpose.
> The budget request included $60,0 million for concept definition for the Navy Theater-Wide program. It is not clear to the committee why this much funding is required for concept definition work. Therefore the committee recommends a reduction of $50.0 million for Navy Theater-Wide concept definition.
> The budget request included $177.0 million for Block II risk reduction efforts, including funds for both S-band and X-band radar technology. The committee is encouraged that the Department of Defense is funding radar technology work for the Navy Theater-Wide program, but is concerned that [BMDO] has not yet decided which radar technology is best suited for ballistic missiles defense.... Therefore, the committee recommends a reduction of $87.0 million for Navy Theater-Wide radar risk reduction efforts.
> The budget request included $260.0 million for Aegis Leap Intercept (ALI) testing of the Block I Navy Theater-Wide interceptor in fiscal year 2002. The committee is encouraged by the strong testing focus, but is concerned about the large increase in the funding for the ALI test program – almost double what was planned last year for fiscal year 2002. A total of five flight tests are planned in 2002 alone. this is a large number for any ballistic missile defense program – more than any other such program has achieved in a single year. Furthermore, the Block I interceptor has had developmental problems that have called into question the reliability and producibility of the interceptor's divert system, which is critical to the missile's ability to hit a target. As such, the likelihood of successfully conducting all five planned flight tests in fiscal year 2002 seem remote. Therefore the committee recommends a reduction of $110.0 million for the Aegis Leap Interceptor testing program. (Pages 215-216)

With reference to a more basic Block I version of the system and a later and more capable Block II version of the system, the committee directed the Secretary of Defense to submit a report to the congressional defense committees no later than April 30, 2002 on the Department's ultimate plans for the Navy Theater-Wide system. The report should indicate whether the Department still plans on pursuing a Block I variant of the system, and if so, provide technical and force structure details on the Block I and a quantitative analysis as to the military value of Block I. The report should also specify the planned date of deployment of the objective (Block II) Navy Theater-Wide system, the technical characteristics of the objective system (e.g., radar and missile type and performance), and the total planned objective force structure of ships and missiles. The report should also provide year-by-year and total life cycle cost estimates for the objective system and separate year-by-year and total life cycle costs for any planned Block I system. (Page 216)

In its report (H.Rept. 107-298 of November 19, 2001) on the FY2002 defense appropriations bill (H.R. 3338), the House Appropriations Committee recommended reducing funding for the Sea-Based Midcourse program by $96 million, stating, "The department [of Defense] has not decided whether to continue this program beyond testing or to pursue one of several alternative missile designs instead. Therefore, the Committee believes it is inappropriate to buy five contingency missiles before the missile has been tested and before the Department has committed to this solution." (Page 249)

Terminal Defense Segment

Ground-Based Terminal
Patriot PAC-3

The Patriot PAC-3 (Patriot Advanced Capability-3, MIM-104 Patriot/ERINT) is the U.S. Army's primary medium-range air defense missile system and is considered a major system improvement over the Patriot used in the Gulf War, and of the subsequent PAC-2. It will target enemy short-and medium-range missiles in their mid-course or descent phase in the lower atmosphere, and will be used in conjunction with the longer-range THAAD. When all changes have been made, the PAC-3 will have a new hit-to-kill interceptor missile (the ERINT), improved communications, radar, and ground support systems. The first unit to be equipped with the final version is to receive PAC-3 missiles in late 3001 at

Fort Bliss, Texas. Full-rate production was scheduled to begin in late 2001, but slipped to late 2002.

In April 2002, the Pentagon projected costs of PAC-3 had increased by $102 million to $2.9 billion because of increased reliability and spares costs. A GAO report issued in July 2000 showed PAC-3 total program costs increased from $3.9 billion for 1,200 missiles planned in 1994 to $6.9 billion for about 1,012 missiles in the current plan. In April 2001, BMDO estimated the PAC-3 acquisition costs to be $10.1 billion. BMDO and the Army are attempting to cut the current cost of the missile to allow the purchase of additional missiles. In December 2000, the Army announced it had restructured the program to finish testing and begin full-rate production earlier. It also plans to increase the numbers purchased in the years 2003-2007. For FY2002, the Bush Administration requested $784 million for PAC-3, a 76% increase over the amounts requested and approved for FY2001. The Administration also transferred funding for the PAC-3 from BMDO to the Army. The House Armed Services Committee, in its version of the FY2002 Defense Authorization Bill did not approve this transfer; this too was later sustained in Congress. Beginning in 1999, PAC-3 had a successful string of intercept flight tests destroying 10 of 11 targets, prior to the test failures in February 2002.

A major concern has been the rising costs of PAC-3. It has been argued that unit costs could be reduced by increasing the number of units purchased and increasing the pace of production. If more countries buy PAC-3, and if the MEADS program is fielded with PAC-3 missiles, unit costs would be further reduced. (Germany, the Netherlands, Japan, Israel, and Taiwan have Patriot systems and are in various stages of upgrading them. South Korea is considering buying Patriots and Germany and Italy are participating in MEADS, which would use Patriot missiles.)

In May 2000, DoD decided to stop development of PACM (designed to defeat cruise missiles) because PAC-3 and improvements being made to PAC-2 systems provide a more cot effective defense against ballistic and cruise missile threats. The decision has been controversial, particularly among companies that would have produced PACM. But the conference report on the FY2001 authorization bill noted no funds had been requested for PACM and instructed the Secretary of Defense to determine if PACM production is warranted.

The effectiveness of PAC-3, and other missile defenses, against countermeasures is also an issue. Russia has developed a guided warhead for the Scud missile that it claims has an accuracy of 10-20 meters, can defeat Patriot missile defenses, and is immune to jamming and electronic countermeasures. It was reported in March 2001 that Russia is offering this warhead for sale to a number of countries in the Middle East that have Scud missiles.

Theater High Altitude Area Defense (THAAD)

The THAAD program is the U.S. Army's weapon system designed to destroy non-strategic ballistic missiles just before they reenter the atmosphere or in the upper atmosphere. The THAAD missile would use a single-stage, solid propellant rocket and a hit-to-kill interceptor designed to destroy the attacking missile with the kinetic energy of impact. Unlike lower-tier, shorter range systems, such as the Patriot PAC-3 and MEADS, THAAD is intended to help protect wider areas against missiles and falling debris of missiles, as well as possible nuclear, biological, or chemical materials.

In April 2000, the Pentagon released a Selected Acquisition Report stating the projected costs of THAAD had increased by $898 million to a total of $9.5 billion because of a revised estimating methodology. In April 2001, BMDO estimated THAAD acquisition costs to be $16.8 billion, and the life cycle costs to be $23 billion.

THAAD entered the Engineering and Manufacturing Development (EMD) phase in late June 2000. A more advanced version designed to defeat attacking missiles employing countermeasures was scheduled for 2011. In an accelerated development proposal the Army considered in 2000, the first THAAD unit equipped could be moved from FY2007 to FY2006. The Department of Defense is still studying this accelerated option. Simultaneously, DoD is relaxing the requirement that THAAD be able to intercept targets within and outside the atmosphere, raising the altitude at which it must be able to conduct an intercept. The minimum intercept altitude had been 40 kilometers.

Earlier technological problems in THAAD's development jeopardized support for the system. But on June 10, 1999, after THAAD had failed in six previous interceptor flight tests, the first success was achieved. In each of those six previous unsuccessful intercept flight tests, a different subsystem had failed. On August 2, 1999, a second THAAD missile successfully intercepted a target missile.

After the second successful intercept, Lockheed Martin submitted a proposal for moving THAAD in EMD, but the Army Space and Missile Defense Command rejected the proposal in April 2000 because of management and testing plan deficiencies. Lockheed Martin addressed these problems, and the Army later recommended the Defense Acquisition Board (DAB) begin its review of THAAD advancing to EMD.

Because of concerns that the THAAD and NTW programs were not being tested against target missiles with the speed and other characteristics of likely enemy missiles (such as the North Korean Taep'o-dong 1), Rep. Vitter introduced legislation in 1999 (H.R. 2596) that would have required BMDO to make appropriate program management and technology adjustment sin the NTW and THAAD programs. Similar legislation in the 107th Congress, such as H.R. 1282, was designed to help NTW and THAAD improve their likelihood of successful intercepts against more realistic test targets.

For FY2002, the Bush Administration requested $922 million for THAAD, which was a 68% increase over the amount requested and appropriated for FY2001 ($549.9 million), and a 32% increase over the amount requested for FY2002 by the outgoing Clinton Administration. Congress cut THAAD funding by $50 million for FY2002. This cut was directed at denying the Administration's request to acquire a limited number of THAAD contingency missiles. The estimated FY2003 request for THAAD is about $1 billion; details will be forthcoming shortly.

Medium Extended Air Defense System (MEADS)

The Medium Extended Air Defense System (MEADS), is a multinational, ground-based, mobile, air and missile defense system. It is essentially a composite of existing technologies with either similar or enhanced capabilities. It will cover the lower-tier of the layered air and theater missile defense and will operate in the division area of the battlefield to protect against various airborne threats. Distinguishing characteristics of MEADS are its stated ability to maneuver and deploy quickly and to provide 360-degree coverage. It will be able to accompany troops within the theater and will require less manpower and logistical support to operate than other missile defense systems. MEADS will use the Patriot PAC-3 missile with its hit-to-kill warhead, designed to intercept multiple and simultaneous short range ballistic missiles (SRBMs), low cross-section cruise missiles and aircraft, and unmanned aerial vehicles. MEADS will eventually replace the aging HAWK air defense system. In addition to fulfilling operational requirements for limited air defense, the program is also expected to reinforce interoperability of NATO forces and to reduce the U.S. burden of cost for helping to maintain European defense.

BMDO has been responsible for program direction and system architecture and integration. The Pentagon sought to shift the management of

MEADS and PAC-3 to the Army from BMDO. Some question whether the Army will give the program sufficient budget priority to sustain development. The House Armed Services Committee did not approve this transfer in its version of the FY2002 Defense Authorization Bill, and this was upheld by Congress.

Under the initial May 1996 Memorandum of Understanding, Germany and Italy committed to fund 25 percent and 15 percent of the program, respectively, for the next 10 years. The German military has questioned the number of MEADS units it would need and whether it could afford them, the German Parliament balked at approving its share of development costs, and the German government then asked to have the program restructured to reduce its $22 billion cost, even if that required reduced capability. In July 2001, the NATO MEADS Management Agency granted a three-year, $216 million risk reduction contract to MEADS International (a team consisting of Lockheed Martin, Alenia Marconi, and the European Aeronautic Defence and Space Company). The United States will pay 55 percent of the risk reduction program, Germany 28 percent, and Italy 17 percent. The agreement was modified to divide German funding and commitment into three phases to ease the Defense Ministry's negotiations with Parliament. Germany has also decided to stop upgrading its Patriot batteries until it can determine whether MEADS will duplicate Patriot's capabilities. The definition phase of development has been extended three years thus putting deployment off till 2009.

Responding to congressional criticism of the program's costs for FY2001, Pentagon officials suggested that Germany and Italy coproduce the Patriot PAC-3 interceptor for incorporation into MEADS. In April 2000 it was reported that Germany and Italy had tentatively agreed to use the Patriot rather than a new interceptor, but still plan to develop a new seeker radar.

For FY2002, the Administration requested $74 million for development of MEADS, $20 million more than was appropriated for FY2001 (the defense authorization act for FY2001 decreased the requested amount by $9.7 million). In the final appropriations bill, funding for MEADS was cut slightly.

The Lockheed-Martin Corp. and the Hughes Aircraft and Raytheon Company consortium represented the U.S. partners of two competing international teams. Alenia of Italy and European Aeronautic Defence and Space Company (formerly Daimler-Chrysler Aerospace) of Germany, represent the European group. In May 1999, the three governments selected the team headed by Lockheed martin to develop MEADS. Target production and fielding dates were set for 2006 but have slipped to 2009.

In May 1996, France rescinded its initial commitment to fund 20 percent of the MEADS program. Despite budgetary constraints, however, France is still interested in developing missile defenses, perhaps an indigenous system. The United Kingdom is not a participant in the program and to date has taken no official position on it. The Netherlands and Turkey have also considered participating in the joint endeavor.

Sea-Based Terminal
Cancellation of NAD Program

On December 14, 2001, DoD announced that it has canceled the Navy Area Defense (NAD) program – the program being pursued as the Sea-Based Terminal portion of the Administration's overall missile-defense effort – due to poor performance, significant cost overruns, and substantial development delays. DoD stated, in announcing the cancellation, that the program's unit acquisition and unit procurement costs had risen 57 percent and 65 percent, respectively.[57]

In announcing the cancellation, DoD cited the Nunn-McCurdy provision, a defense-acquisition law passed in the 1980s. Under the law, a major defense acquisition program experiences what is called a Nunn-McCurdy unit cost beach when its projected unit cost increases by at least 15 percent. If the increase reaches 25 percent, the Secretary of Defense, to permit the program to continue, must certify that the program is essential to national security, that there are no alternatives to the program that would provide equal or greater military capability at less cost, that new estimates of the program's unit acquisition cost or unit procurement cost appear reasonable, and that the management structure for the program is adequate to control the program's unit acquisition or unit procurement cost.

Edward C. "Pete" Aldridge, the Under Secretary of Defense for Acquisition, Technology and Logistics – the Pentagon's chief acquisition executive – concluded, after examining the program, that he could not recommend to Secretary of Defense Donald Rumsfeld that he make such a certification. Rumsfeld accepted Aldridge's recommendation and declined to issue the certification, triggering the program's cancellation. This was the

---

[57] Acquisition cost is the sum of procurement cost plus research, development, test and evaluation (RDT&E) cost.

first time that a defense acquisition program had been canceled as a result of a decision to not certify under a Nunn-McCurdy unit cost breach.[58]

DoD stated that the cancellation of the program "will result in a work stoppage at some government and contractor facilities." Major contractors for the NAD program were Raytheon of Tucson, AZ, Lockheed Martin of Moorestown, N.J. and Middle River, MD, United Defense of Baltimore, MD, and Minneapolis, MN, Orbital Sciences of Dulles, VA and Chandler, AZ and L-3 Communications of New York, NY. Major government field activities involved in the program were the Naval Surface Warfare Center (NSCWC) at Dahlgren, VA, NSWC at Port Hueneme, CA, the Applied Physics Laboratory of John Hopkins University of Laurel, MD, and Lincoln Laboratories of the Massachusetts Institute of Technology of Lexington, MA.

The cancellation of the program will result in about $300 million in contract-termination costs. Congress, acting on the FY2002 defense budget in the week following the announcement of the program's cancellation, reduced the Administration's request for the program to $100 million, leaving about $200 million in contract-termination costs apparently unfunded.[59]

DoD officials have stated that although the NAD program has been canceled, the requirement for a sea-based terminal system remains intact. DoD and the Navy are now exploring options for a potential replacement program. If pursued, a replacement program could resemble the original NAD program in some respects, and perhaps many. One option that may be considered would combine the booster stages (the "back end") of the SM-2 Block IV A missile that was being developed under the NAD program with the guidance section and KKV (the "front end") of the Army's PAC-3 terminal-defense missile.[60]

---

[58] Navy Area Missile Defense Program Cancelled. Department of Defense News Release No. 637-01, December 14, 2001; Dao, James. Navy Missile Defense Plan Is Canceled By the Pentagon. *New York Times*, December 16, 2001; Ratnam, Gopal. Raytheon Chief Asks DoD To Revive Navy Program. *Defense News*, January 14-20, 2002: 10.

[59] Weinberger, Sharon. Cancellation Of Navy Area TMBD Ends Advanced Intercept Work, Leaves DOD Owning Termination Fees. *Aerospace Daily*, December 18, 2001; Woods, Randy. Congress Provides No Money For Canceled Area Missile Defense. *Inside the Navy*, December 24, 2001.

[60] Weinberger, Sharon. Pentagon To Consider Resurrecting Navy Area Missile Defense Program. *Aerospace Daily*, December 20, 2001; Sirak, Michael. US DoD Studies Army Technology for Navy Missile. *Jane's Defence Weekly*, January 2, 2002: 8; Ratnam Gopal. Study Begins On Ways For Navy To Retake Missile Role. *Defense*

Background on the Now-Cancelled NAD Program

The NAD program, also sometimes called the Navy Lower Tier program, was initiated several years ago. Prior to DoD's December 14, 2001 cancellation announcement, the Bush Administration's plan was to maintain the mission and system configuration of the NAD program as originally defined, but transfer the program from BMDO (now MDA) to the Navy on the grounds that the program was technically more mature and had evolved from an air defense mission.

The NAD program was to have been deployed on Navy Aegis ships and was designed to intercept short- and medium-range theater ballistic missiles (TAMS) in the final, or descent, phase of flight, so as to provide local-area defense of U.S. ships and friendly forces, ports, airfields, and other critical assets ashore. The program involved modifying both the Aegis ships' radar capabilities and the standard SM-2 Block IV air-defense missile fired by Aegis ships. The missile, as modified, was called the Block IVA version.[61] The system was designed to intercept descending missiles within the Earth's atmosphere (endo-atmospheric intercept) and destroy them with the Block IVA missile's blast-fragmentation warhead.

Sensors Segment

The sensors program element includes funding for the Space-Based Infrared System-Low (SBIRS-Low); the Russian-American Observation Satellite, or RAMOS (an international cooperative project to develop new missile early warning sensor technology); and program operations. For FY2003, the request is $294 million for SBIRS-Low, $69 million for RAMOS, and $10 million for program operations, a total of $373 million. According to the House Armed Services Committee's press release on its markup of the FY2003 DoD authorization bill (H.R. 4546), the committee approved $373 million.

Of these projects, SBIRS-Low is the most visible and controversial. It is one component of the Space Based InfraRed System (SBIRS), which is designed to replace and enhance the capabilities of existing satellites that

---

News, January 7-13, 2002: 8; Keeter, Hunter. Service Officials: Navy Terminal-Phase Missile Defense Remains Requirement. *Defense Daily*, January 18, 2002: 2.

[61] The modifications include a new, thrust-vector-controlled booster, a stronger airframe, the addition of a dual-mode radio frequency/infrared [RF/IR] guidance sensor, an improved blast-fragmentation (i.e., explosive) warhead, and enhancements to the missile's autopilot-control system.

provide early warning of missile launches. Historically, U.S. early warning satellites have been placed in geostationary orbit, high above the equator (22,300 miles). SBIRS also will use satellites in that orbit, as well in highly elliptical orbits, and in low orbits. Hence, the SBIRS program is divided into two components: SBIRS-High and SBIRS-Low. For more on both SBIRS-High and SBIRS-Low, see CRS Report RS21148. SBIRS-High is managed by the Air Force and will not be discussed further here. Management of SBIRS-Low was moved from the Air Force to the Ballistic Missile Defense office (now the Missile Defense Agency) effective Oct. 1, 2001 to emphasize that its primary objective is to support missile defense.

The mission of SBIRS-Low[62] is to track missiles from launch to intercept or reentry; discriminate between targets and decoys; transmit data to boost, midcourse and terminal defense systems that will cue radars and provide intercept handovers; and provide data for intercept hit/kill assessments.

Because of deep concerns about the technological readiness of SBIRS-Low, and escalating cost projections, Congress appropriated no funding for SBIRS-Low in Fy2002 ($385 million had been requested). However, it appropriated $250 million for "Satellite Sensor Technology" and gave the Secretary of Defense discretion a to whether the funding should be spend on SBIRS-Low or other technologies. The decision was to continue with a restructured SBIRS-Low program.

On April 15, MDA Director General Ronald Kadish submitted the restructuring plan to Congress. The SBIRS-Low design last year envisioned a system consisting of between 20 and 30 satellites in low Earth orbit (the exact number had not been finalized). The first launch was projected for 2006. FY2003 DoD budget materials indicated that the launch would slip to 2008, but under the April 15 restructuring plan, two demonstration satellites will be launched beginning in FY2006 or FY2007. MDA is using its "spiral development" strategy for SBIRS-Low and these two research and development (R&D) satellites will have less capability than what was ultimately envisioned. In the late 1990s, DoD planned to launch three demonstration satellites, called the Flight Demonstration System (FDS), but terminated that effort in 1999 due to rising costs. Now, DoD is returning to the demonstration satellite approach. Sensors and flight structures built for the FDS satellites will be used for the R&D satellites identified in the

---

[62] MDA, FY2003 RDT&E budget justification (R2-A Exhibit, Project 5041), available at: [http://www.dtic.mil/comptroller/fy2003budget/budget_justification/index.html].

restructuring plan. According to that plan, new technologies will be introduced as they mature, with incremental improvements in satellite lifetimes, focal plane arrays, and cryocoolers, for example.

Because the program recently was restructured, and there is no final system architecture, cost estimates are problematic. The General Accounting Office (GAO) reported[63] in February 2001 that DoD, using the system description at the time, estimated the life-cycle cost for SBIRS-Low through FY2022 was $11.8 billion. A January 2002 Congressional Budget Office (CBO) report[64] estimated the cost through 2015 at $14-17 billion (of which $1 billion was appropriated prior to FY2002). In its report on the FY2002 DoD appropriations bill, the House Appropriations Committee reported (H.Rept. 107-298, p. 250) that the program's life cycle cost had grown from $10 billion to over $23 billion. The April 15 restructuring plan did not include a new DoD cost estimate, but said that out-year funding estimates would be developed as part of the FY2004-2009 FYDP. At an April 17, 2002 hearing before the Senate Appropriations defense subcommittee, MDA director General Kadish reported that additional funds are expected to be needed to FY2002 and FY2003. According to a press report,[65] the figure for FY2002 is $13 million.

Two industry teams were chosen in 1999 for program definition and risk reduction (PDRR). The Spectrum Astro/Northrop Grumman team included Boeing, Lockheed Martin, and others. The TRW/Raytheon team included Aerojet Motorola, and others. DoD had been expected to select one of the teams for the next phase (EMD) in mid-2002. However, as part of the April 15 restructuring plan, DoD decided to merge the two teams. TRW was named the prime contractor, and Spectrum Astro a major subcontractor, for the satellites. Competition at the sensor subcontractor level will continue, though, with Raytheon and Northrop Grumman pursuing independent parallel sensor development to demonstrate on-orbit performance with the series of R&D satellites.

The February 2001 GAO report raised questions over whether SBIRS-Low could meet its technical milestones. GAO concluded that five of six critical satellite technologies were too immature to ensure they would be ready when needed: the scanning infrared sensor, tracking infrared sensor, fore optics cryocooler, tracking infrared sensor cryocooler, and satellite

---

[63] U.S. General Accounting Office. Space-Based Infrared System-Low at Risk of Missing Initial Deployment Date. Washington, GAO, February 2001. GAO-01-06. p. 3.
[64] Congressional Budget Office. Estimated Costs and Technical Characteristics of Selected Missile Defense Systems, Jan. 2002 [http://www.cbo.gov].
[65] Aerospace Daily, April 18, 2002, p. 1.

communications crosslinks. GAO also cited concurrency as a concern in that satellite development and production were scheduled to occur at the same time; the results of an on-orbit test would not be available until 5 years after the satellites entered production; and software would be developed concurrent with the deployment of the satellites and not be completed until more than 3 years after the first SBIRS-Low satellites were launched. Other critics cite the ability to discriminate between targets and decoys, and the ability to share information between satellites, as significant technical hurdles.[66]

The House Appropriations Committee, reporting on the Fy2002 DoD appropriations bill (H.Rept. 107-298, p. 250), cited a not-yet-released internal DoD study on ground- and sea-based alternatives to SBIRS-Low. The committee reported that the DoD study indicates ground based radars are a viable, lower cost, and lower risk, alternative. In the April 15 SBIRS-Low restructuring plan, MDA stated that it is investigating multiple sensor technologies in parallel, including land-, sea-, air-, and space-based platforms. It will evaluate the alternatives to determine the best sensor mix for meeting BMDS needs.

RECENT CONGRESSIONAL ACTION

FY2002

FY2002 Authorization

The House Armed Services Committee (HAS) approved the Administration's request for $8.3 billion for ballistic missile defense, making only minor adjustments in funding (H.R. 2586). The Committee disapproved, however, of DoD's proposal to transfer terminal defense programs – PAC-3, MEADS, and Navy Area Defense from BMDO to the services because of concern that the services would not adequately fund those programs.

During House debate over the FY2002 defense authorization bill, an amendment offered by Rep. Stump was adopted. It would reduce BMDO funding by $265 million, and transfer that money to counterterrorism and

---

[66] Robbins, *op cit.*

intelligence programs. Specifically, $145 million would be taken from the Mid-Course Segment and $120 million from the Boost Phase Segment.

The Senate Armed Services Committee (SAC) recommended several major changes to funding and management of ballistic missile defense in the FY2002 defense authorization bill (S. 1416).

- Establishing a new requirement that would prohibit spending for any missile defense activities that would conflict with the ABM Treaty (as determined by the President) would be contingent on Congress voting to approve such expenditures under special expedited procedures; and

- Reducing BMD funding by $1.3 billion on the basis that funding was premature or insufficiently justified, including major cuts to the following programs:
    - Airborne laser (-$80 million in a $410 million program);
    - Navy Theater-wide (-$347 million in a $596 million program);
    - Ground-based mid course system (-$330 million in a $3,231 million program);
    - Space Based Infrared system – Low (SBIRS-Low) (-$97 million in a $3895 million program); and
    - THAAD (-$210 million in a $909 million program; and

- Permitting DoD to reorganize the funding of ballistic missile defense into large, aggregated program elements but requiring new reporting requirements on individual programs; and

- Allowing DoD to transfer three programs previously funded by the Ballistic Missile Defense Organization (BMDO) to the individual services (i.e., PAC-3 (Army), MEADS (Army), Navy Area Defense (Navy)), as well as the transfer of three Air Force programs to BMDO.

The restriction on funding of activities that would violate the ABM Treaty was highly controversial because the President signaled that he would veto the DoD Authorization Act if that provision were included.

After the terrorist activity on September 11th, Senator Levin, Chairman of the SAC, indicated that he would transfer that ABM Treaty-related restriction from the DoD authorization bill to a separate bill. This was done the week of September 22, when a new bill (S. 1438) was introduced to replace S. 1416.

The bill passed by the Senate, S. 1438, removed the controversial sections requiring congressional approval of activities that would violate the ABM Treaty, as well as certain reporting requirements for BMD programs. Those sections were put in S. 1439, a separate bill that was filed at the same time. The rest of S. 1438 is the same as S. 1416 (the bill that was reported by the SAC). Senators Levin and Warner offered an amendment to S. 1438 to restore the $1.3 billion cut from missile defense programs for: 1) RDT&E for missile defense; and 2) activities for combating terrorism. The President would be given discretion as to how to allocate these funds. This amendment was adopted by unanimous consent.

FY2002 Appropriations

The Senate Appropriations Committee included $8.3 billion for missile defense program, and, as with the Senate authorization bill, permitted the President to reallocate $1.3 billion of this total to combat terrorism. The Senate approved this as well. The House Appropriations Committee approved $7.9 for ballistic missile defense programs, but transferred these programs to a new, separate appropriations title "Counter-terrorism and weapons of mass destruction." This was approved by the House.

In conference, $7.77 billion was approved. House and Senate conferees gave their support to Defense Department efforts to devise a management structure to facilitate integration of research and development, but cautioned against implementing a process that might limit adequate oversight by various Pentagon review groups and Congress. Finally, conferees agreed with House language that identified several special interest projects for purposes of reprogramming and budget justification material: Terminal Phase Systems (MEADS and ARROW); Midcourse Phase Systems (Ground-based Midcourse, Pacific Test Bed, and Sea-based Midcourse); Boost Phase Systems (Sea-based Boost, Air-based Boost, and Space-Based Boost); and Sensors (Satellite Sensor technology and RAMOS.

FY2003

In early February 2002, Defense Secretary Rumsfeld announced that the Administration would ask for $7.8 billion for missile defense spending for FY2003. But when the Missile Defense Agency provided Congress details of its budget, the amount requested was considerably less ($6.7 billion). As they did last year, the Pentagon is seeking to remove the PAC-3 program and funding for it from the MDA to the Army. The amount for PAC-3 EMD (Engineering, Manufacturing, and Development) and procurement is $812 million. Therefore, the combined total request for missile defense spending for FY2003 is about $7.5 billion, and is the most accurate number. The Pentagon has not provided an explanation of why there was a difference between $7.8 and $7.5 billion.

As broken down, this year's request for:

- the Terminal Defense segment request if for $1.1 billion (or $1.9 billion when you include PAC-3)
    - $66 million for Arrow
    - $958 million for THAAD EMD
    - $90 million for Sea-based Terminal
    - $14 million for program operations

- the Midcourse Defense segment request is for $3.19 billion
    - $534 million for the Test Bed
    - $2.07 billion for the Ground-based Midcourse program
    - $427 million for the Sea-based Midcourse program
    - $160 million for program operations

- the Boost Defense segment request is for $797 million
    - $90 million for Sea Boost
    - $598 million for Air Boost
    - $54 million for Space Boost
    - $35 million for the Space Based laser
    - $20 million for program operations

- the Sensors segment request if for $373 million
    - $294 million for SBIRS-Low
    - $69 million for RAMOS
    - $10 million for program operations

- the BMD System program request is for $1.1 billion

In its version of the FY2003 Defense Authorization Bill (H.R. 4546), the House Armed Services Committee approved $7.784 billion for ballistic missile defense. It returned responsibility for MEADs program and the PAC-3 program to the Missile Defense Agency (MDA), and added an additional $21 billion to the Administration's request for missile defense.

Chapter 2

NATIONAL MISSILE DEFENSE: ISSUES FOR CONGRESS

Steven A. Hildreth and Amy F. Woolf

SUMMARY

Many in Congress and outside the government have shown strong interest in deploying a ballistic missile defense to protect the United States from attack. The ABM Treaty prohibits nationwide defense but permits the United States to deploy up to 100 interceptors for long-range ballistic missiles at a single site. Many supporters of National Missile Defense (NMD) argue that the United States must amend or abrogate this treaty so that it can pursue a more robust defense.

The United States has pursued the development and deployment of defenses against long-range ballistic missiles since the early 1950s. It deployed a treaty-compliant site in North Dakota in the mid-1970s, but shut it down after only a few months of operation. President Reagan launched a research and development effort into more extensive defenses in the early 1980s, but these plans were scaled back several times during the Reagan and Bush Administrations. The Clinton Administration initially focused NMD efforts on technology development, but, in 1996, outlined a strategy to pursue the development and deployment of an NMD system by 2003 if the threat warranted and the technology was ready. In January 1999, the Administration announced that it had adjusted this program to permit deployment in 2005, and would decide in Summer 2000 whether to proceed with deployment of up to 20 at a single site. This was modified in February 2000 to allow for 100 interceptors. The Bush Administration favors a more robust NMD program that is likely to include land, sea and space-based assets. The President emphasized his Administration's commitment to missile defenses in a speech on May 1, 2001.

Secretary Powell, Secretary Rumsfeld, and the President have all highlighted this commitment during meetings with allies in Europe.

Many in Congress disagreed with the Clinton Administration's approach arguing that the threat justified the more rapid deployment of an NMD system. Other analysts argued that the United States should modify a Navy theater missile defense system so that it would have the capability to defend against long-range ballistic missiles. Still other maintain that the United States should focus on arms control and nonproliferation strategies, rather than missile defenses, to counter the threats from missile proliferation. The Clinton Administration identified several factors regarding deployment of an NMD system. Technically, these still guide the program. These included an assessment of the threat to the United States form long-range ballistic missiles, an assessment of the maturity of the technology and the feasibility of deploying an effective system, consideration of the implications for the ABM Treaty and the possibility of gaining Russian agreement on amendments, the potential costs of the prospective system, and the environmental implications of deployment. Many in Congress questioned the Administration's commitment to NMD funding and deployment. Some argued that additional funds could have speeded the development and deployment of the program. And, in an effort to press the Administration to deploy an NMD, both the House and the Senate passed legislation on NMD deployment. With the Congress and the White House controlled by the Republican Party, NMD advocates anticipate congressional approval of the likely Bush plan.

MOST RECENT DEVELOPMENTS

On June 12, 2001, during his first visit to Europe, President Bush stated that "the ABM Treaty is a relic of the past." He added that it "prevents freedom-loving people from exploring the future. And that's why we've got to lay it aside."

The Bush Administration still has not outlined any details of its prospective missile defense architecture, or any specific intentions to withdraw from the ABM Treaty. However, in meetings with NATO defense ministers in Brussels on June 7, 2001, Secretary of Defense Rumsfeld emphasized that the Administration would press ahead with the development of missile defenses and that scrapping of the ABM Treaty was "inevitable" because it constrained both testing and deployment of missile defenses.

The Secretary also indicated that the Administration might seek to deploy a rudimentary missile defense system quickly, before the end of the President's first term in 2004. He acknowledged that this system would not be fully tested and might not be very effective, but he emphasized that it would be a first step in the U.S. effort to discourage rogue nations from acquiring and threatening the United States with long-range ballistic missiles. Many Members of Congress, including the new chair of the Senate Armed Services Committee, Carl Levin, have opposed this approach. Senator Levin has stated that the United States should continue with research and development for missile defenses, but that it should not deploy anything until a system had been fully tested and proven to work.

On June 1, President Bush submitted a formal request to Congress for supplemental appropriations for FY2001, but it did not include additional funds for NMD as many had predicted. Some in Congress may attempt to add such funds, but that has not yet happened and it is unclear how the Administration might respond.

INTRODUCTION

Many in Congress and outside government have a strong interest in deploying a ballistic missile defense (BMD) system to protect the United States from attack. The collapse of the Soviet Union in 1991, Iraq's use of Scud missiles in the 1991 Persian Gulf War, and the proliferation of ballistic missile technologies, all added to concerns about the risks to the United States. Two events in the summer of 1998 served to amplify these concerns. First, in July, a congressionally-mandated panel chaired by former Secretary of Defense Donald Rumsfeld (now Defense Secretary again) concluded that nations seeking to develop long-range ballistic missiles might be able to achieve that objective within 5 years of deciding to do so, and that the United States might have little warning before the testing and deployment of such missiles. And, second, at the end of August, North Korea flight tested a 3-stage ballistic missiles. Although the third stage of this missile apparently failed in flight, and this missile would not have had the range to reach the continental United States, North Korea demonstrated that it had developed the technology for "staged" missiles, a milestone considered critical to the development of longer-range ballistic missiles.

Both the Clinton Administration and Congress reacted to these developments. In January 1999, the Administration announced that, for the first time, it had allocated funding in its Future Years Defense Plan (FYDP) for the deployment of a National Missile Defense (NMD) system, even though it would not decide whether to deploy such a system until Summer 2000. And, in March 1999, Congress passed by a wide margin legislation declaring it the policy of the United States to deploy an NMD.

This chapter provides an overview of the current debate on NMD. It begins with a brief summary of the provisions of the 1972 ABM Treaty and a short history of U.S. NMD efforts. It then reviews approaches to NMD development and deployment, describing current NMD strategy and major alternative views on how the United States should address missile threats to its territory. The chapter then identifies and describes the factors that the Clinton Administration considered in its September 2000 decision to delay NMD deployment. Finally, the chapter summarizes current debate in Congress about NMD, focusing on budget issues and legislation.

THE 1972 ANTI-BALLISTIC MISSILE (ABM) TREATY

The 1972 U.S.-Soviet Anti-Ballistic Missile (ABM) Treaty prohibits the deployment of ABM systems for the defense of the nations' entire territory. It permits each side to deploy limited AMB systems at two locations, one centered on the nation's capital and one at a location containing ICMB silo launchers. A 1974 Protocol further limited each nation to one ABM site, located either at the nation's capital *or* around an ICBM deployment area. Each ABM site can contain no more than 100 ABM launchers and 100 ABM interceptor missiles. The Treaty also specifies that, in the future, any radars that provide early warning of strategic ballistic missile attack must be located on the periphery of the national territory and oriented outward. The Treaty bans the development, testing, and deployment of sea-based, air-based, space-based, or mobile land-based ABM systems and ABM system components (these include interceptor missiles, launchers, and radars or other sensors that can substitute for radars).

HISTORY OF NMD IN THE UNITED STATES

The Sentinel and Safeguard Programs

The United States has pursued research and development into anti-ballistic missile (ABM) systems since the early 1950s. In the mid-1960s it developed the Sentinel system, which would have used ground-based, nuclear-armed interceptor missiles and would have been deployed around a number of major urban areas to protect against Soviet attack. In 1969, the Nixon Administration renamed the system "Safeguard," and changed its focus to deployment around offensive missile fields, rather than cities, to ensure that these missiles could survive a first strike and retaliate against the Soviet Union. The Senate almost approved an amendment halting construction of the system in 1969, but the program continue when Vice President Agnew broke a tie vote. Nevertheless, sentiment against ABM deployments and in favor of negotiated limits on AMB systems was growing. The United States and Soviet Union concluded negotiations on the ABM Treaty in 1972. The United States completed its ABM site near Grand Forks, North Dakota. It operated for 9 months in 1974 and 1975, then was shut down because it proved to be not cost-effective. Russia continues to operate a modernized ABM site around Moscow. U.S. research and development into ABM systems, especially for ICBM protection, continued, albeit at lower budget levels through the late 1970s, before rising again during the Carter Administration.

The Strategic Defense Initiative (SDI) and Global Protection Against Limited Strikes (GPALS)

In March 1983, President Reagan announced an expansive effort to develop non-nuclear ballistic missile defenses that would protect the United States against a full-scale attack from the Soviet Union. Although the Strategic Defense Initiative (SDI) remained a research and development effort, with little testing and no immediate deployments, President Reagan and the program's supporters envisioned a large-scale defensive system with thousands of land-, sea-, air-, and space-based sensors and interceptors. As cost estimates and technical challenges increased, the Reagan Administration announced it would begin with more limited deployment of land-based and space-based sensors and interceptors that would seek to disrupt, rather than defeat, a Soviet attack. The former Bush Administration further scaled back the goals for U.S. missile defense programs, in part as a result of the demise of the Soviet Union and the changing international political environment. Instead of seeking to protect the United States against a large-scale attack, the United States would seek to deploy a defensive system that could provide Global Protection Against Limited Strikes (GPALS). This type of ballistic missile defense would have sought to protect the United States, its forces, and allies against an accidental or unauthorized attack from the Soviet Union or an attack by other nations who had acquired small numbers of ballistic missiles.

National Missile Defense (NMD) TechnologyDevelopment Program

After the 1993 Bottom Up Review (a DOD-wide review of U.S. military plans and programs), the Clinton Administration decided to emphasize theater missile defense (TMD) development and deployment efforts, and to focus NMD on technology development. Secretary of Defense Les Aspin noted that these program changes reflected an assessment that the regional ballistic missile threat already existed, while a ballistic missile threat to the United States *per se* might emerge only in the future. Many in Congress disagreed with this assessment and continued to press for the development and deployment of an NMD system. In 1996, the Clinton Administration adopted the 3+3 strategy to guide the development and potential deployment of an NMD system that could defend the United States against attacks from small numbers of long-range ballistic missiles. This strategy envisioned continued development of NMD technologies during the first 3 yeas (1997-2000), and, if the system were technologically feasible and warranted by prospective threats, deployment in the second three year period (2000-2003). The Administration modified its strategy in January 1999 by adding $6.6 billion to the FY1999-2005 FYDP to support the possible deployment of an NMD system and moving the planned deployment date from 2003 to 2005. But the Administration emphasized than an NMD deployment decision still would not be made until Summer 2000. On September 1, 2000, President Clinton announced that he had decided **not** to authorize deployment of a National Missile Defense (NMD) system at this time because he did not have "enough confidence in the technology, and the operational effectiveness of the entire NMD system." Research and development would continue, as would discussions with the Russians about modifications to the ABM Treaty, but the planned deployment date would slip until 2006 or 2007. The President further stated that the final decision on deployment would be left to the next Administration.

APPROACHES TO NMD

Clinton Administration Program

Program Design and Architecture

The Clinton Administration granted a contract to Boeing North America to serve as the "lead system integrator" for the NMD program. Boeing serves as the prime contractor, and will integrate elements of the program developed by different companies into an NMD system. Boeing also will execute the test program. (Boeing has contracted to provide 20 GBIs for deployment, as well as five spares. It must also build another 14 missiles for flight tests prior to deployment, and another 36 for follow-on test and evaluation flights.)

BMDO initially described 3 notional architectures: C1 (Capability 1); C2; and C3. The C1 architecture might deploy up to 20 interceptors at one site to defend against a very limited threat, such as a small-scale accidental or unauthorized launch, or a small-scale deliberate attack. President Clinton's September 2000 decision against deployment would delay this initial system by a year or two. Currently, the FYDP provides funding for 100 interceptors and the support sensor and weapon infrastructure. This new architecture has been called C-1 Prime.

As of today, the prospective NMD system architecture still consists of: 1) the Ground-Based Interceptor, which includes a booster rocket, kill vehicle, and ground-based command and launch equipment; 2) a Ground Based Radar that will perform acquisition, tracking, discrimination, and kill-assessment functions; 3) the Battle Management, Command, Control, and Communications system that will be used to identify and assess attacks and authorize the launch of interceptor missiles; 4) and space-based sensors for early warning of attack (i.e., Defense Support Program/Space Based Infrared System and the Space and Missile Tracking System/Space Based Infrared System Low Earth Orbit). Other candidate sensors include Upgraded Early

Warning Radars, which will provide enhanced capability for the United States to detect and track missile launches, as well as other radars.

Congressional Reaction to the Clinton Administration Program

Many in Congress disagreed with the Clinton Administration's NMD strategy. Some argued that the threat form uncertainties in Russia and missiles in rogue nations exists now. Some also argued that the United States may have too little warning to respond to emerging threats with the deployment of a missile defense system. And some argued that the Clinton Administration placed the ABM Treaty above U.S. national security, maintaining it at all costs in spite of the demise of the Soviet Union. And many were particularly concerned about the Administration's refusal to commit to deploy an NMD system immediately. Conversely, some, including Senator Biden, argued that the new NMD strategy represents a turning away from long-term U.S. arms control objectives and nonproliferation policy.

After the Clinton Administration altered its NMD program in January 1999, some Members praised the Administration for adding deployment funds to the budget. Senator Jon Kyl stated, "I'm delighted. I think reality finally caught up with them." But some continued to question the Administration's commitment to NMD and they expressed concerns about the delay in the deployment date. For example, Representative Curt Weldon said he remained skeptical because the program still lacked a firm commitment to deployment and Senator Robert Smith noted that he did not see a commitment to deployment that matched the rhetoric from the Administration. Nevertheless, in the report that accompanied the Senate Armed Services Committee's version of the FY2000 Defense Authorization Bill (S.1059), the committee praised the Administration for fully funding the development and deployment of an NMD system.

A few Members of Congress argued previously that the Clinton Administration's approach to NMD would have provided too little protection against the range of threats faced by the United States. Some would like to see a program that includes space-based sensors and interceptors. Others believe a sea-based NMD can provide more robust coverage sooner and for less money than the Administration's program (this concept is discussed below). And some Members believe that the United States should continue to pursue the development of a missile defense that can protect the United

States from a large-scale attack by Russia. They note that Russian missiles still threaten the United States, and changes in Russian leadership could restore the adversarial relationship between the two nations.

Despite the failed intercept in July 2000, congressional sentiment appeared to support efforts to continue keeping the program on track and pushing forward with a summer 2000 deployment decision. However, a growing number of Members had argued that President Clinton should delay the decision until the next Administration. When the President announced such a delay on September 1, 2000, many Members praised his move. Most Democrats and some Republicans appeared to agree that the technology had not yet proved to be feasible and that further testing should be completed before a final deployment decision. Some Republicans, however, viewed the President's announcement as further evidence that the Clinton Administration was not serious about missile defense and had done little to protect the American public. Senator Trent Lott referred to the decision as "another example of the Clinton-Gore Administration's legacy of missed opportunities." Representative Curt Weldon stated that the President's "misguided decision" would leave Americans "completely unprotected against the weapon of choice for rogue nations and terrorist groups – the missile."

Prospective Bush Administration Plan

The Bush Administration initiated a full review of the NMD program in mid-February 2001. On May 1, 2002, he outlined his Administration's approach to missile defense in a major speech. The President emphasized that his Administration was committed to the development of missile defenses, and, although these defenses would be too limited to undermine Russia's nuclear forces, they would be far more extensive than those planned by the Clinton Administration. The Bush Administration plans to pursue defenses based on land, at sea, and in space, and to seek boost-phase, mid-course, and terminal intercept capabilities. The President did not announce that the U.S. is prepared to withdraw from the ABM Treaty, but he indicated that the Treaty was out of date and that the United States would move beyond its constraints when developing its missile defense technologies. He called on Russia to join the United States in developing a new framework for strategic stability and international security that would replace the Cold War model of deterrence through nuclear retaliation with a new model that included both offensive and defensive capabilities in deterrence.

Secretary of Defense, Donald Rumsfeld, outlined the Administration's general goals for missile defense in a speech at the Munich Conference on European Security Policy. At that event he stated that the United States intends to develop and deploy a missile defense designed to defend or people and forces against a limited ballistic missile attack..." He said that the United States wold consult with its allies about this deployment and that it had "every interest in seeing that our friends and allies... are defended from attack." Secretary Rumsfeld offered further support for the Administration's missile defense policies during meetings with NATO defense ministers in early June 2001. He offered the allies briefings that reportedly highlighted the growing threat from ballistic missile proliferation and emphasized that the United States would build a system of "layered defenses" involving ground, sea and space-based weapons to cope with a growing threat of ballistic missile sin the hands of unpredictable forces. He also stated that the need to move beyond the ABM Treaty was "inescapable."

Reports indicated that the Bush Administration is exploring alternatives that would allow the quick deployment of a rudimentary missile defense system before the end of the President's first term in 2004. The lead contractor for national missile defense, Boeing, has outlined an alternative that would allow the United States to deploy a small number of interceptor missiles at a site in Alaska, without the completion of the X-Band radar at Shemya, in that time frame. Secretary Rumsfeld has indicated that such a system would not be fully tested and may not even be very effective, but it would represent a first step in the deployment of a layered defense system.

Critics of this approach argue that the system would represent a "scarecrow" that would do nothing to protect the United States but would require the near-term withdrawal from the ABM Treaty. Some also argue that this system could undermine U.S. nonproliferation goals, by encouraging nations to acquire missiles and threaten the United States sooner, rather than later, while the defensive system remained so simple and limited. Members of Congress have also criticized this approach. Senator Carl Levin, the new chair of the Senate Armed Services Committee has stated that he supports research and development on missile defense, but that the United States should not deploy a system until it is fully tested and proven to work.

Sea-Based NMD

Some NMD supporters, and increasingly senior Navy military leaders, have advocated an alternative sea-based NMD program. The Heritage Foundation, for instance, examined current and future ballistic missile threats in 1995 and 1996 and proposed a sea-based NMD to meet these threats. The Foundation's most recent (March 1999) report, *Defending America: A Plan to Meet the Urgent Missile Threat*, outlined a plan "to achieve the most cost effective, most affordable global anti-missile protection in the shortest time." The plan, supported by other conservatives as well, calls for deploying an NMD system based aboard the U.S. Navy's Aegis ships. Currently the United States has about 27 Aegis cruisers and about 26 Aegis destroyers (by about 2008, there will be 57 destroyers).

There was some movement in 1999 on this issue. In the report that accompanied the Senate Armed Services committee's version of the FY2000 Defense Authorization Bill (S.1059), the Committee called on the Secretary of Defense to prepare a new report evaluating options for supplementing a land-based NMD architecture with sea-based assets. It mandated that the report address the engineering steps that would be needed to develop a sea-based NMD system and that it evaluate requirements, performance benefits, design trade-offs, operational impacts, and refined cost estimates for sea-based NMD assets. Meanwhile, the Navy has proceeded to examine more closely some of the many technical and cost hurdles. But a recent, comprehensive review ("*Taking National Missile Defense to Sea: A Critique of Sea-Based and Boost-Phase Proposals*,") counters supporters' claims that a sea-based NMD system would be inexpensive and easy to deploy quickly [http://www.clw.org/ef/seanmd.html].

Boost-Phase NMD

By mid-2000, a growing number of analysts and critics of the Administration's NMD program, from across the political spectrum, had begun to argue that the United States should pursue boost-phase, rather than mid-course ballistic missile defenses. A boost-phase defense would attack an enemy's missiles early in flight, before they had left the atmosphere and before they had time to deploy multiple warheads or decoys. The interceptors could be deployed at sea, on land, or in space, as long as they were close enough to intercept an enemy's missiles within the first few minutes of its launch. Some critics, such as Richard Garwin, argued that this type of defense would be the only way to protect the United States against missile attack because a land-based, mid-course NMD would not be able to distinguish between decoys and actual warheads. Others, including then Governor George Bush, argued that the United States should pursue boost-phase defenses as a part of a more robust system, because that would give the United States multiple opportunities to intercept attacking missiles.

Officials in Russia have also argued for the development of boost-phase defenses. In early June, President Putin proposed that the United States and Russia cooperate on the development of boost-phase defenses that could "put a cap" on rogue nations and their missiles. He also proposed that Russia share its technology for these missiles with nations in Europe. He stated that this type of defense would not violate the ABM Treaty because it could be directed against theater-range ballistic missiles. The Clinton Administration was skeptical of the Russian proposal because it lacked details. Furthermore, the Clinton Administration argued that this would not replace the U.S. NMD program because it could not protect against long-range strategic ballistic missiles.

The Clinton Administration did not deny the potential for boost-phase defenses for NMD, but noted that the technologies for this type of system were not as advanced as the technologies for mid-course defenses, and that the United States would not be able to deploy such defenses until years after the current 2005 goal for NMD deployment. Furthermore, some critics have argued that, because the defenses would have to respond instantaneously to the launch of an enemy missile, the United States would have to trust computers, rather than human beings, to interpret events and initiate a conflict.

Focus on Arms Control and Nonproliferation Strategies

Some Members of Congress and analysts outside government argue that the United States does not need a national missile defense to address the threat of missile attack from rogue nations. Some believe that the United States will not be able to develop and deploy a cost-effective NMD because of daunting technical challenges and certain high costs that would be associated with such a complex weapon system. Others argue that rogue nations with weapons of mass destruction could attack the United States with lower cost, and less obvious, means than ballistic missiles. They note that a

BMD system would do nothing to stop cargo ships, small aircraft, or other unconventional or simpler means of delivery. Some also argue that a U.S. NMD could actually intensify missile threats to the United States if Russia slows or stops its offensive force reductions in response to U.S. proposals for changes in the ABM Treaty. They note that the strategic arms reduction treaties will eliminate thousands of warheads that could destroy the United States, while an NMD would only attempt to defend against a few dozen warheads.

Most critics of proposals to deploy an NMD do not dispute that some nations hostile to the United States may be seeking long-range ballistic missiles. They would, however, address these threats with a combination of diplomatic, arms control, and nonproliferation tools. They believe that economic, political, and military incentives, could help persuade nations not to pursue missile technologies or sell them to countries of concern. And they argue that a strong international nonproliferation regime could bring more pressure to bear on rogue nations than a U.S. NMD. And if cooperative methods are less than successful, many note that the United States could still deter missile attacks from rogue nations with its overwhelming military superiority in nuclear and conventional forces. They believe that no nation, even one led by a leader with less-than-rational objectives, would risk attacking the United States if it believed that its own survival would be threatened in response.

FACTORS AFFECTING AN NMD DEPLOYMENT DECISION

The Clinton Administration identified four broad criteria to consider in its Deployment Readiness Review: an assessment of the threat, an assessment of the arms control and strategic environment, a technical assessment of the program, and an assessment of the cost of the NMD system. Additionally, however, an environmental impact assessment was prepared. these are discussed further below. The degree to which these may be applied to NMD deployment plans in the Bush Administration has not been made clear.

Threat Assessment

In 1995, Intelligence Community concluded in its November 1995 report, *Emerging Missile Threats to North America During the Next 15 Years, NIE 95-19*, that "no country, other than the major declared nuclear powers, will develop or otherwise acquire a ballistic missile in the next 15 years that threaten the contiguous 48 states." Some Members of Congress disputed this finding, noting that it did not address threats to Alaska and Hawaii, and did not consider the possibility that nations might accelerate missile program by buying technologies, or full missile systems, from other nations. Some in Congress argued that the Administration had directed the report's findings to support the slow pace of its NMD program. Congress mandated that an independent panel review the underlying assumptions and conclusions of NIE 95-19. This panel, known as the Gates Commission, noted that the study may have been conducted in haste and that its conclusions were politically naïve because they did not examine the entire range of issues associated with foreign missile developments. However, it concluded that the study had not been politicized with a result directed by the White House.

In 1997, the intelligence community reaffirmed that the United States would not face a new long-range missile threat for 10-15 years. Members of Congress, however, continued to question this conclusion, and in the FY1997 Defense Authorization Act, Congress mandated that the CIA appoint an independent panel to review the emerging missile threat to the United States. In July 1998, this panel, chaired by former Secretary of Defense Donald Rumsfeld (now Defense Secretary again), reported that a threat to the United States could emerge sooner than 2010, and that countries such as North Korea or Iran might have long-range missiles within 5 years of deciding to develop such systems. In January 1999, the Clinton Administration appeared to accept the Rumsfeld Commission's conclusions. Secretary Cohen noted that "there is a threat, and the treat is growing, and... it will soon pose a danger... to Americans here at home." He highlighted North Korea as a potential source of this threat.

At around the same time, the intelligence community appeared to alter its assessment of the threat from North Korea. In late 1998, Robert Walpole, the National Intelligence Officer for Strategic and Nuclear Programs, spoke about the results of an assessment completed in October 1998. This study concluded that North Korea's Taepo Dong II missile, which is still under development, might have the range needed to reach most of the United States, albeit with an inaccurate and very light payload. And, in testimony before Congress in late February 1999, General Lester Lyles, the Director of the Ballistic Missile Defense Organization, stated that North Korea might acquire that capability by the year 2000. The Director of Central Intelligence, George Tenet, also noted in testimony in February that North Korea's Taepo Dong II missile might have the capability to reach Alaska and Hawaii with a larger warhead and the rest of the United States with a smaller, inaccurate warhead.

In early September, 1999, the intelligence community released a new estimate of the projected ballistic missile threat to the United States. This report indicates that Russia, China, and North Korea are all likely to have ICBMs that can reach U.S. territory in the next 15 years, that Iran probably will have such a capability, and Iraq possibly may have that capability. The report indicated that Russia will have the most robust force, but, because of economic constraints, its force levels are likely to decline below the levels permitted by existing arms control agreements. China may also have tens of missiles armed with nuclear warheads that could target the United States, and that the Chinese threat would, in part, be influenced by technology gained through espionage. The report also stated that North Korea might test its Taepo-Dong II missile at any time, and that this missile could have the capability to deliver an early-generation nuclear weapon to U.S. territory. The Taepo-Dong I missile, which was tested in August 1998, might reach U.S. territory, but only with a lighter chemical or biological weapons payload, and with significant inaccuracies.

Technical Feasibility

The meaning of technical feasibility as a criteria for deployment has been relatively open to interpretation. In the NMD debate, it generally carries two meanings. First, there is a political connotation. Many in Congress and elsewhere who want an NMD system deployed as soon as technologically possible tend to believe that this criteria would be met as soon as the United States develops and tests all the components of a prospective system. This generally means that when a system can be built, it should be built. A second meaning of technical feasibility refers to specific criteria established with the Defense Department in order for a weapon system to proceed toward deployment. Until recently, these included a number of precise and technical criteria to be achieved within the program before a positive recommendation for NMD deployment could be made to the White House.

The NMD program office in the Pentagon has stated that two successful test intercepts will be required to move the program forward. Site construction contracts can be awarded after one successful intercept, but two successes must be achieved before actual site construction can begin. Additionally, a new NMD milestone was established called the "site authority to proceed." This requires that the Secretary of Defense authorize the start of site construction in April 2001 based on the decisions the United States has made regarding the ABM Treaty. (A decision at this time is necessary to meet the scheduled 2005 NMD fielding date.) Last year, the number of flight tests that could occur before the Deployment Readiness Review (DRR) was reduced from four to three. The pace of the program has caused senior technical experts in and outside of the Pentagon to warn that significant program risk exists, which could lead to negative program developments down the road. They warn that the program is being scheduled, rather than event driven.

Recent intercept attempts confirm that unambiguous success remains elusive. On October 2, 1999, BMDO reported it had successfully intercepted an intercontinental ballistic missile over the Pacific Ocean. Reportedly, the test demonstrated the "hit-to-kill" technology being pursued in the current NMD program. But, reports of test anomalies surfaces in Jan. 2000, which DOD officials confirmed were true, but who argued nonetheless that the kill vehicle "worked in spite of that." On January 18, 2002, a second test failed to destroy its target over the Pacific Ocean as planned. Defense officials pointed out, however, that other test objectives such as system integration were achieved. Preliminary analyses suggested that the two infrared sensors on the kill vehicle failed in the last seconds of the test, causing it to miss the target. Then, on July 7, 2000, the kill vehicle failed to separate from the booster rocket, so the test of its capabilities never occurred.

In February 2000, additional criticism of the NMD program surfaced from within the Pentagon's Operational Test & Evaluation directorate, warning of undo pressure placed on the NMD program to meet an artificial decision point in the development process. This echoed similar criticism from a November 1999 Pentagon sponsored panel of technical and national security experts (the Welch panel). Some critics outside the government have focused on the system's ability to discriminate between warheads and decoys on an attacking missile. They note that adversaries are likely to deploy decoys in an effort to defeat the system, and, therefore, the system will be ineffective as soon as it is deployed. Some conclude that this weakness means the United States should not proceed with the development and deployment of NMD; others conclude that the United States should pursue more robust and advanced NMD technologies, including advanced space-based sensors and boost-phase interceptors.

By July 2000, a growing number of analysts and Members of Congress had called on the Clinton Administration to delay its NMD deployment decision. Some argued that the technology had not proven feasible; others wanted the decision to be made by a new President in January 2001. In late August, 2000, Philip Coyle, the Director of Operational Testing at the Department of Defense, stated that the United States would not be able to deploy an NMD system by the target date of 2005 because testing of the system's components had fallen behind schedule. He contended that a more aggressive testing program would be needed to achieve a deployment date of 2005.

By late July and early August, reports indicated that Secretary of Defense Cohen was likely to advise the President to proceed with early steps in the contracting process for the construction of the X-band radar in Alaska. This construction would have to begin by Spring 2001 to support a 2005 deployment date. But the process could be stopped, before construction began, if the next President decided to pursue a different path on NMD. However, President Clinton did not accept this recommendation, and, when he announced that he would not authorize deployment of an NMD system, he cited the test failures and questions about technical feasibility as his primary concerns.

Arms Control and Strategic Environment

In January 1999, Secretary of Defense Cohen stated that NMD deployment "might require modifications to the [ABM] Treaty and the Administration is working to determine the nature and scope of these modifications." In late February 1999, Deputy Secretary of State Strobe Talbott met with Russian officials in Moscow to begin discussions about ABM Treaty modifications. The U.S. team sought to reassure Russia that the planned NMD would not interfere with Russia's strategic nuclear forces and that the United States will views the ABM Treaty as central to the U.S.-Russian strategic balance. The Russians were reportedly unconvinced, and continued to argue that the United States overstated the threat from rogue nations so that it could build a defense capable of intercepting Russian missiles. When discussions resumed in mid-August 1999, the two sides again reaffirmed that the Treaty is the "cornerstone of strategic stability," but

Russian officials continued to reject the idea that the treaty could be amended and argued that any changes to the treaty would upset strategic stability, undermine Russia's national security, and undermine the whole offensive arms control process. In November 1999, President Yeltsin warned that any U.S. attempt to move beyond the existing limits in the ABM Treaty would "have extremely negative consequences" for other arms control treaties.

In February 2000, Secretary of State Albright reported a slight change in Russia's response to U.S. proposals after meetings with then-acting President Putin. However, the Russian position remained firm throughout the year. When the Russian parliament approved ratification of the START II Treaty in April 2000, it indicated that U.S. withdrawal from the ABM Treaty could be considered an extraordinary event that would lead to Russia's withdrawal from START II. Furthermore, in June 2000, Defense Minister Sergeyev repeated Russia's contention that the U.S. NMD system could be easily expanded and, therefore would undermine Russia's nuclear deterrent. He argued that the United States would use its NMD system along with its offensive forces to achieve superiority over Russia and China. Presidents Clinton and Putin discussed ABM Treaty issues at their summit meeting in Moscow in June 2000. However, they made little progress on resolving their differences. In a Joint Statement on the Principles of Strategic Stability, they agreed that the ABM Treaty remains the "cornerstone of strategic stability," but that it could be modified in response to changes in the international security environment. They also agreed that the international community faces a growing threat from the proliferation of weapons of mass destruction, but Russia did not agree that this justified any change in the ABM Treaty.

President Clinton sited the continuing impasse with Russia on AMB Treaty modifications when he announced that he would not proceed with NMD deployment at the present time. A delay in the start of construction at Shemya Island would, according to the President, give the United States more time to pursue discussions with Russia in n effort to "narrow our differences" on the nature of threat and the U.S. interest in NMD. In late November, 2000, President Putin stated that Russia would be willing to reduce its offensive forces below 1,500 warheads if the United States remained committed to the ABM Treaty. This proposal was unlikely to break the deadlock because the United States had shown little interest in such deep reductions in offensive forces, and U.S. officials have stated that the United States would only accept Russian proposals for deep cuts if Russia were to accept U.S. proposals to modify the ABM Treaty.

Although the Bush Administration has indicated that it would discuss U.S. NMD plans with Russian officials, it has not set an agenda or a timeline for negotiations on modifications to the ABM Treaty. Officials in the Administration have, however, referred to the ABM Treaty as "ancient history" and "no longer relevant to the new strategic environment." Through these and other comments, Administration officials have signaled a willingness to withdraw from the ABM Treaty if Russia is unwilling to modify it ore replace it with an agreement that would permit the deployment of more robust defenses. Some analysts believe that a U.S. announcement of withdrawal would compel Russia to agree to modifications; others argue that Russia's acquiescence or opposition is not important because the United States should simply proceed with the defenses it deems necessary.

In addition to considering the arms control objectives, U.S. officials have also considered the effect that NMD deployment would have on relations with NATO allies and China. Within these countries there is little enthusiasm for the United Stated deploying an NMD system, and in some cases (including NATO countries), there are strong negative reactions. President Clinton also acknowledged the opposition from U.S. allies when he announced his decision not to proceed with NMD deployment, noting the United States must have allied support because key components of the system would be on their territories. He expressed a willingness to consult with U.S. allies about NMD, even though his Administration did not begin these consultations until months after it began to plan for NMD deployment.

President Bush has also recognized that China and U.S. allies have expressed opposition to NMD. Officials from the Administration have simply stated that china has nothing to fear from U.S. NMD because it would not be directed against china's missiles. The Administration has, however, taken a more active role in consulting with U.S. allies about NMD and in ensuring the allies that the United States would include them in its missile defense efforts. Initially, this active effort appeared to have eased the allies' concerns. President Bush spoke with several European and NATO leaders prior to his May 1, 2001 speech on missile defense, and he sent several delegations to Europe and Asia after the speech to consult with the allies about missile defenses. However, these consultations did not win widespread support for the Administration's position. Officials in many NATO nations have argued that the Administration's representatives offered few details of the U.S. plans for a missile defense architecture and failed to answer questions about the new strategic framework envisioned by the Administration. They also have not seen or heard any details about the effect that their concerns might have on the Administration's plans. When Secretary of State Powell attended a meeting of NATO Foreign Ministers at the end of May, he failed to convince the allies to accept the U.S. view of emerging ballistic missile threats. Then, during meetings with NATO defense ministers, Secretary of Defense Rumsfeld appeared to indicate that the United States was prepared to move forward with missile defense deployments and withdrawal from the ABM Treaty regardless of the concerns expressed by other nations, including the NATO allies. Hence, officials in many NATO countries have questioned whether the Administration's approach included "real" two-way consultations with the allies or simply sought to inform the allies of U.S. intentions.

Budget Issues

There has never been a clear, consensus cost figure for deploying an NMD system. For several years, the Clinton Administration estimated that a limited NMD system would cost $9 to $11 billion to develop, test, and deploy. In January 1999, the Administration estimated that an initial system of 20 interceptors would cost about $10.6 billion. In February 2000, the Administration provided a life-cycle cost estimate of $26.6 billion for an initial system of 100 ground-based interceptors, presumably in Alaska. A couple of months later, the Pentagon provided a life-cycle estimate of $30.2 billion for the NMD system ($FY1991). By May 2000, the General Accounting Office reported a cost figure of $36.2 billion (GAO/NSIAD-00-131), which number MBDO also apparently was using.

A late April 2000 study by the Congressional Budget Office (CBO) estimated that it would cost about $29.5 billion to develop, build, and operate an initial NMD system (the expanded Capability I system) through 2015. This total cost was comparable to the Administration's estimate of $30.2 billion (now apparently $36.2 billion). CBO estimates it will cost another $19 billion through 2015 to expand the initial system of 100 interceptors and build what is called a Capability 2 and Capability 3 system designed for greater numbers of more sophisticated potential missile threats. Additional space-based sensors would bring the total costs of NMD to around $60 billion through 2015. NMD critics argue that the true costs will be even higher, perhaps as much as $120 billion, to include other items some NMD supporters want: space-based and naval-based NMD interceptors.

Environmental Issues

In November 1998, the Administration filed a Notice of Intent in the *Federal Register* that MBDO would begin to hold public scoping hearings in conjunction with its plan to conduct an environmental impact analysis of potential locations for elements of an NMD system (*Federal Register* 63915-16). Thus far, these locations include only Alaska and North Dakota, with Alaska being chosen for the first place.

The purpose of the public scoping hearings was to gather information from interested parties regarding specific environmental concerns. This input was considered in a draft Environmental Impact Statement (EIS). More public meetings were held prior to the final EIA in the spring of 2000.

In late September 1999, the draft EIS was reported to include language for a possible two-site deployment of NMD interceptors – Alaska and North Dakota. It suggested that up to 100 interceptor silos could be located in one location or up to 100 could be deployed in both one site in Alaska or North Dakota. This appears to represent a change from the original focus on one NMD site.

NMD IN CONGRESS

Budget Issues

Despite the addition of $6.6 billion to the FYDP starting in FY2000 for NMD deployment, some continued to express doubts about the Clinton Administration's commitment to NMD. Some supporters argued that an NMD system could be deployed earlier than 2005 if the Administration allocated more money. But program managers in DOD and BMDO believed little more could be done without introducing significant program risk. Time and engineering effort, not more money, will lead to effective NMD development as soon as possible, according to this view. An additional $2.2 billion was added to the FYDP in FY2001. Figures for the Bush Administration budget have not been announced.

Legislative Debate

No action has been taken on the Bush missile defense budget because those numbers have not been announced. Although many in Congress disagreed with the Administration's plans for NMD, they were not able to enact legislation that would mandate the deployment of nationwide ballistic missile defenses until March 1999. President Clinton vetoed the Defense Authorization Bill for FY1996, in part, because it contained such a mandate. In 1996 and 1997 Congress considered, but failed to pass, independent legislation that would mandate the deployment of an NMD system. On April 21, 1998, the Senate Armed Services Committee approved the American Missile protection Act of 1998 (S. 1873, S.Rept. 105-175). This legislation called for the deployment of a national missile defense system as soon as the technology was ready. When the bill came to the floor in May 1998, Democrats succeeded with a filibuster. The effort to invoke cloture failed by one vote, 59 to 41, with only 4 Democrats joining all 55 Republicans in support of the legislation. The Senate failed, again, to invoke cloture, in a vote held on September 9, 1998. Once again, the vote was 59-41.

Senator Cochran introduced this bill again in January 1999 (S. 257). After failing to win changes in the language, the Administration reportedly threatened to veto the legislation because it would only use the state of technology as the measure for deployment, and would ignore considerations about cost, threat, and treaty-compliance. Nevertheless, the Senate Armed Services Committee approved the legislation, by a vote of 11-7, on February 9, 1999. The full Senate approved the bill, by a vote of 97-3, on March 17, 1999. Democrats dropped their opposition to the Senate bill, and the White House withdrew its threat of a veto, after the Senate approved an amendment stating that it is U.S. policy to continue to negotiate with Russia on reductions in offensive nuclear weapons and an amendment noting the NMD programs remained subject to annual authorization and appropriations for funding.

Representative Curt Weldon introduced similar legislation in the House on August 5, 1998 (H.R. 4402) and, again, in early February 1999 (H.R. 4). This legislation simply states that it is "the policy of the United States to deploy a National Missile Defense." Although it does not specify when or how much missile defense the United States should deploy, supporters argued that it would produce a major change in U.S. policy because although Administration policy at the time supported development, it left a deployment decision for the future. This legislation passed the House Armed

Services Committee, by a vote of 50-3, on February 25, 1999, and the full House, by a vote of 317-105, on March 18, 1999.

The Senate took up H.R. 4 on May 18, 1999. It struck all but the enacting clause with the language of S. 257, then approved the modified bill by unanimous consent. The House debated the new version of H.R. 4 on May 20, 1999, and approved the bill with the Senate language by a vote of 345-71. Congress sent the legislation to the President on July 12, 1999, and the President signed it on July 23. Some Members of Congress were angered by the Administration's interpretation of the legislation. They noted that the Administration was not prepared to implement the law because it still planned on deciding whether to proceed with NMD deployment after the program review in Summer 2000. Members, including Representative Weldon, argued that the legislation eliminated the need for this decision by indicating that the United States would proceed with deployment as soon as the technology was ready. Yet, in a statement issued when he signed the law, President Clinton noted that "by specifying that any NMD deployment must be subject to the authorization and appropriation process, the legislation makes it clear that no decision on deployment had been made."

Chapter 3

NATIONAL MISSILE DEFENSE: RUSSIA'S REACTION

Amy F. Woolf

SUMMARY

In the late 1990s, the United States began to focus on the possible deployment of defenses against long-range ballistic missiles. The planned National Missile Defense (NMD) system would have exceeded the terms of the 1972 Anti-Ballistic Missile Treaty. Recognizing this, the Clinton Administration sought to convince Russia to modify the terms of the Treaty. But Russia was unwilling to accept any changes to the Treaty. It also decried the U.S. plan to deploy NMD, insisting that it would upset strategic stability and start a new arms race.

Russia has claimed that the ABM Treaty is the "cornerstone of strategic stability" and that, without its limits on missile defense, the entire framework of offensive arms control agreements could collapse. Furthermore, Russia argues that a U.S. NMD system would undermine Russia's nuclear deterrent and upset stability by allowing the United States to initiate an attack and protect itself from retaliatory strike. The Clinton Administration claimed that the U.S. NMD system would be directed against rogue nations and would be too limited to intercept a Russian attack. But Russian officials question this argument. They doubt that rogue nations will have the capability to attack U.S. territory for some time, and they believe that the United States could expand its NMD system easily. Furthermore, they argue that, when combined with the entirety of U.S. conventional and nuclear weapons, an NMD system would place the United States in a position of strategic superiority.

Russian officials have stated that, if the United States withdraws from the ABM Treaty and deploys an NMD, Russia would withdraw from a range of offensive arms control agreements. Furthermore, Russia could deploy multiple warheads on its ICBMs to overcome a U.S. NMD, or deploy new intermediate-range missiles or shorter-range nuclear systems to enhance its military capabilities.

Russia has also outlined diplomatic and cooperative military initiatives as alternatives to the deployment of a U.S. NMD. Russia has proposed that the international community negotiate a Global Missile and Missile Technology Non-Proliferation regime as a means to discourage nations from acquiring ballistic missiles. It has also suggested that it would cooperate with nations in Europe to develop and deploy defenses against theater-range ballistic missiles. Many analysts believe this proposal was designed to win support among U.S. allies for Russia's opposition to the U.S. NMD program. U.S. officials expressed an interest in the idea but said it could not substitute for defenses against longer-range missiles.

The Clinton Administration sought to address Russia's concerns by offering continued support to the fundamental principles of the ABM Treaty and by seeking to convince Russia that the U.S. NMD system would remain too limited to threaten Russia's nuclear deterrent. The Bush Administration, in contrast, has supported more robust missile defenses, but it also has stated that they will not be directed against Russia's offensive forces. The President has indicated that the United States will need to move beyond the limits in the ABM Treaty, but he suggested that Russia join the United States in developing a new strategic framework.

INTRODUCTION

During the latter years of the Clinton presidency, the United States began to focus on the possible deployment of defenses against long-range ballistic missiles. The Administration, and many missile defense supporters, claimed that the United States needed to pursue National Missile Defenses (NMD) because "rogue" nations such as North Korea, Iran, and Iraq might soon acquire longer range missiles that could strike U.S. territory, and the United States could not be certain that the threat of offensive retaliation would deter these unpredictable actors. The Clinton Administration realized that its plans for NMD would exceed the limits imposed by the 1972 Anti-Ballistic Missile Treaty between the United States and Soviet Union. Consequently, the Administration opened discussions with Russia in an effort to negotiate amendments to the Treaty that would permit the deployment of a limited NMD system.

Russian officials have consistently and repeatedly insisted that the 1972 AMB Treaty is the cornerstone of strategic stability (this is defined on page 4). They have argued that any changes to the Treaty that permitted the deployment of defenses against long-range ballistic missiles would undermine international strategic stability, upset the nuclear balance established by the Treaty, and interfere with Russia's nuclear deterrent capabilities. Russia has, thus far, refused to accept any modifications to the ABM Treaty that would permit national missile defenses and has campaigned against the U.S. policy at meetings with other nations and international organizations. Russia has also offered alternatives, suggesting that the United States, Russia, and the international community address emerging missile threats with diplomacy and arms control measures that would seek to stop the proliferation of new threats and with cooperation on theater-range ballistic missile defenses to address those threats that did emerge.

This report provides a detailed review of Russia's reaction to U.S. policy on NMD and U.S. proposals for modifications to the ABM Treaty. It begins with a brief background section that describes the central limits in the ABM Treaty and U.S. policy on the deployment of NMD. It then describes, in more detail, Russia's objections to the U.S. proposals. The report also provides a summary of possible military responses that Russia might take if the United States were to abrogate the ABM Treaty and begin deployment of missile defenses and contains a discussion of Russia's proposals for diplomatic and military alternatives to the U.S. plans to deploy missile defenses. The report concludes with a brief discussion of the U.S. response to Russia's objections and a few issues for Congress.

BACKGROUND

The ABM Treaty

The United States and Soviet Union signed the Treaty on the Limitation of Anti-Ballistic Missile Systems (ABM Treaty) in May 1972. This Treaty prohibits the deployment of ABM systems for the defense of the nations' territory, or an individual region, or defenses that can provide the base for such a defense. It permits each side to deploy limited ABM systems at two locations, one centered on the nation's capital and one at a location containing ICBM silo launchers. A 1974 Protocol further limited each nation to one ABM site, located either at the nation's capital *or* around an ICBM deployment areas. Each ABM site can contain no more than 100 ABM launchers and 100 ABM interceptor missiles The Treaty also specifies that, in the future, any radars that provide early warning of strategic ballistic missile attack must be located on the periphery of the national territory and oriented outward.

The Treaty bans the development, testing, and deployment of sea-based, air-based, space-based, or mobile land-based ABM systems and ABM system components (these include interceptor missiles, launchers, and radars or other sensors that can substitute for radars). Each party can propose amendments, and, in the Standing Consultative Commission established by the Treaty, they can consider possible proposals for further increasing the viability of the Treaty. Each party can also withdraw from the Treaty, after giving 6 months notice, if "extraordinary events related to the subject matter of this Treaty have jeopardized its supreme interests."[1]

In September 1997, the Clinton Administration signed a Memorandum of Understanding on Succession that named Russia, Ukraine, Belarus, and Kazakhstan as the successors to the Soviet Union for the Treaty. This agreement has never entered into force because Congress insisted that the Clinton Administration submit it to the Senate for advice and consent, as an amendment to the Treaty. The Clinton Administration never did so, in part because it feared that the Senate might reject the agreement in an effort to abolish the Treaty. Some Members of Congress have argued that the ABM Treaty is no longer in force because the Soviet Union has ceased to exist.

---

[1] For the full text of the Treaty and a description of the process leading to its negotiation see Arms Control and Disarmament Agreements. Texts and Histories of the Negotiations. United States Arms Control and Disarmament Agency. Washington, D.C. 1990.

The Clinton Administration, however, determined that, in the absence of alternative arrangements, Russia would serve as the successor to the Soviet Union for the Treaty.

The Bush Administration has not explicitly accepted the argument that the ABM Treaty is no longer in force and Deputy Secretary of Defense Wolfowitz has said the United States would withdraw before violating the Treaty. However, during their nomination hearings, Secretary of Defense Rumsfeld referred to the Treaty as "ancient history: and Secretary of State Powell stated that the Treaty is no longer relevant to our strategic framework. President Bush has also said that the ABM Treaty is outdated, and that the United States must move beyond the limits in the Treaty to deploy effective missile defenses.

National Missile Defense Plans

Clinton Administration

The Clinton Administration's plan for NMD, which it outlined in 1999, called for the deployment of 100 interceptor missiles at a single site in Alaska.[2] This system would have been designed to defend against a relatively limited threat of perhaps 20 missiles. Eventually the system might have expanded to 200-250 interceptors at one or more sites to defend against a larger and more sophisticated threat. It might also have included space-based sensors and components currently banned by the ABM Treaty. The Administration recognized that this site, and some of the technologies under consideration, would not have been consistent with the limits in the ABM Treaty. As a result, it participated in discussions with Russia in an effort to modify the ABM Treaty to permit a limited deployment. It would, however, have retained many of the central features of the Treaty that limit the capabilities of ABM systems.

President Clinton announced on September 1, 2000 that he had decided not to authorize deployment of an NMD system because he did not have "enough confidence in the technology, and the operational effectiveness of the entire NMD system." In two of three tests, the defensive missile had

---

[2] For a detailed discussion of the U.S. NMD program and policy towards the ABM Treaty, see U.S. Library of Congress, Congressional Research Service, National Missile Defense: Issues for Congress, CRS Issue Brief IB10034. By Steven A. Hildreth and Amy F. Woolf.

failed to intercept its target. The Administration announced that it planned to continue with research and development on its NMD technologies, and that it would continue discussions with the Russians about the ABM Treaty. But the final decision on whether to begin NMD deployment would be left to Clinton's successor.

Bush Administration

President Bush has emphasized that he places a high priority on defenses that could protect the United States, its forces, and its allies from ballistic missile attack. He outlined his Administration's approach in a speech on May 1, 2001,[3] when he indicated that "we can draw on already established technologies that might involve land-based and sea-based capabilities to intercept missiles in mid-course or after they re-enter the atmosphere."[4] During hearings before Congress in July 2001, Deputy Secretary of Defense Wolfowitz provided more details on the Administration's missile defense program. He stated that the Pentagon would pursue a robust research and development program into a wide range of technologies that could be based on land, at sea, or in space. He stated that the Administration had not yet identified a specific architecture for its system because it would make use of the most promising technologies as soon as they were ready. Ultimately, though, the Administration is seeking to develop and deploy an integrated, layered system that can defend the United States, its forces, and allies from missiles of all ranges at all phases of their flight trajectories.

Administration officials acknowledge that its many part of its missile defense program systems would not be consistent with the terms of the ABM Treaty. They have argued that it should be replaced by a new framework for deterrence that combines both offensive and defensive capabilities. The Administration has not yet announced U.S. withdrawal from the ABM Treaty, but the President and others have stated that they would do so if consultations with Russia on a new strategic framework do not soon produce an agreement to "set aside" the Treaty.

---

[3] The Bush Administration uses the phrase "missile defense" rather than the Clinton-era "national missile defense" to describe the systems currently under consideration. This is a broader concept for missile defense that could combine defenses against both shorter, medium, and longer-range missiles in an integrated defense architecture.

[4] George W. Bush Delivers Remarks on Missile Defense. Transcript. Federal Document Clearing House. May 1, 2001.

THE RUSSIAN RESPONSE

Concerns about Strategic Stability and Arms Control

The dominant theme in Russia's response to the U.S. approach to NMD and the ABM Treaty is the idea that the ABM Treaty is the "cornerstone of strategic stability" and that the U.S. deployment of NMD would undermine stability and upset arms control.[5] According to this view, the Treaty, with its ban on widespread ballistic missile defenses, underscores the Cold War model of deterrence, where neither the United States nor Soviet Union could threaten an attack on the other without facing an overwhelming retaliatory strike. The assured destruction promised by this retaliatory strike meant that the strategic balance was stable, that neither side would risk an attack no matter how grave a crisis. Accordingly, the deployment of ballistic missile defenses that would protect all U.S. territory (as opposed to the limited defenses permitted by the Treaty) would undermine this concept of stability. If a nation could intercept missiles launched in retaliation, particularly if it had diminished their numbers in its initial strike, it might believe it could launch a first strike without fearing retaliation. Knowing this, the nation without the defensive system might conclude that it had to launch preemptively before losing any of its forces in an initial attack. Under these circumstances, stability would be lost because a nation might have an incentive to launch first in a crisis.

Furthermore, Russian officials argue that the ABM Treaty is the cornerstone of the entire network of agreements that reduce offensive nuclear weapons.[6] The Treaty's limits on ballistic missile defenses allowed

---

[5] Russia's former defense minister, Igor Sergeyev, has said "The [1972] ABM Treaty, is the cornerstone for strategic stability and the basis for the system of international agreements in the sphere of the monitoring and control of weapons. Now it has been threatened due to the fact that the USA has decided upon the deployment of a national ABM system, which is prohibited by the [ABM] Treaty... If such a system is deployed in the USA, it [the treaty] will become meaningless. See Russian Defense Minister Sergeyev on Military Reform, Chechnya, ABM Defense. Vek. February 23, 2001. Translated in FBIS Document CEP20010301000351.

[6] Russia's President Putin has said, "People must realize that the mutual reduction of strategic attack weapons – the most dangerous of all nuclear weapons – is possible only when the ABM Treaty continues to hold. Scrapping it would make a further reduction of strategic attack weapons according to START-I impossible. START-II would not come into force either, as it would be impossible to conclude START-III,

the United States and Soviet Union to accept limits and reductions in their offensive forces because they knew they could maintain an effective deterrent at lower levels when the offensive forces could not be blunted by defensive systems. Accordingly, if the United States were to abrogate the ABM Treaty to deploy ballistic missile defense, Russia might feel compelled to abrogate agreements on offensive forces so that it could retain an arsenal of sufficient size to ensure that it could penetrate the U.S. ballistic missile defenses.

Finally, Russian critics note that the U.S. approach to missile defenses and the ABM Treaty would upset not only strategic stability between the United States and Russia, but also international strategic stability. They argue that other nations, such as China, might believe that their offensive forces would be undermined by U.S. defenses, and might feel compelled to expand their arsenals to ensure an effective retaliatory attack. But, if one nation, such as China, were to react this way, other nations might feel threatened and might react, themselves, by increasing their offensive military capabilities. Hence, the deployment of a U.S NMD and U.S. abrogation of the ABM Treaty could set off a new, threatening international arms race. Russian critics, and many critics of missile defense in the United States argue that, in the long run, the United States could become less secure with NMD than it is in its current more "vulnerable" condition.

The Clinton Administration sought to reassure Russia about its concerns for strategic stability. On several occasions, when President Clinton met with President Yeltsin or President Putin, he signed statements and declarations acknowledging that the ABM Treaty remained the cornerstone of strategic stability. At their summit meeting in June 2000, Presidents Clinton and Putin signed a Joint Statement on Principles of Strategic Stability. In this document, the Presidents declared that "They agree on the essential contribution of the ABM Treaty to reductions in offensive forces, and reaffirm their commitment to that Treaty as the cornerstone of strategic

---

aimed at talking about the radical reduction of nuclear arsenals. This blow would also affect other agreements that are of fundamental, global importance: the NPT, and the Nuclear Test Ban Treaty... Russia will be forced to look for an alternative to end its commitments not only regarding START, but also the agreement on intermediate-range and short-range missiles, the conclusion of which is linked to the legal and military framework of the START-II-ABM process." See Gafron, Georg and Kai Diekmann. Russia is Still a World Power. Interview with Russian President Vladimir Putin Hamburg Welt am Sonntag. June 11, 2000. Translated in FBIS Document EUP20000611000121.

stability."[7] At the same time, the United States sought to convince Russia that the Treaty could serve this purpose even if it were modified or amended to allow the deployment of a limited NMD.[8] In addition, the Clinton Administration argued that the changes it sought in the ABM Treaty would permit only a limited NMD system that would address the emerging threat from "rogue" nations and that the system would not be capable enough to intercept the larger numbers of missiles that Russia would possess, even as its forces declined in the coming decade.

Concerns about the Scope and Intent of NMD

Differing Threat Assessments

Russian officials have agreed with the U.S. view that ballistic missile proliferation could pose a problem and introduce new missile threats to both nations. The Joint Statement on Principles of Strategic Stability, signed after the June 2000 summit, stated that the Presidents agreed "that the international community faces a dangerous and growing threat of proliferation of weapons of mass destruction and their means of delivery, including missiles and missile technologies..." Furthermore, the Presidents agreed that "this new threat represents a potentially significant change in the strategic situation and international security environment."[9] In an interview held shortly before the summit, President Putin proposed that the United States and Russia cooperate on the development of a "boost-phase" theater missile defense system that could be based near "rogue" nations to address this emerging threat.[10]

However, Russian officials disagree with the U.S. view that missile proliferation and the potential missile capabilities of "rogue" nations pose a significant or immediate threat to the United States. In an interview with the

---

[7] Joint Statement By the Presidents of the United States of America and The Russian Federation on Principles of Strategic Stability. The White House. Office of the Press Secretary. June 4, 2000.

[8] Secretary of Defense Cohen noted that, although the Presidents agreed that the Treaty remained a cornerstone of strategic stability, it was not a static document. He pointed out that "the treaty allows amendments to fit new strategic realities, such as the emerging new threats we face." DOD News Briefing, Secretary of Defense William S. Cohen, Presenter. June 9, 2000.

[9] Joint Statement By the Presidents. Op cit.

[10] Grier, Peter. Putin's "Star Wars" Lite: Could it Fly? Christian Science Monitor. June 8, 2000, p. 2.

Russian press, President Putin acknowledged that "such threats, theoretically, in principle, [could] emerge one day." But he went on to state that "we do not believe that there are such threats now nor that they are coming from any specific states."[11] Consequently, President Putin did not agree with the U.S. view that these emerging threats justified the U.S. proposals for changes to the ABM Treaty and the deployment of an NMD system.[12] Moreover, Russian officials claim that, even if "rogue" nations could threaten the United States with long-range missiles, the overwhelming power of U.S. offensive forces would deter such an attack. Russia's former Defense Minister, Igor Sergeyev, outlined this view when he stated:

> the development of ICBMs entailed a colossal strain on the economy even for giants like the USSR and the United States. So assertions that ICBMs will appear in the near future in the possession of Third World states that do not possess a sound economy or the relevant technologies appear very lightweight and unfounded. Indeed, even if we imagine the purely theoretical situation where such missiles will become part of the armory, the nuclear deterrence factor that demonstrated its effectiveness back in the Cold War years will still apply to those countries.[13]

Thus, Minister Sergeyev, and other in Russia have concluded that, if the emerging missile threats in "rogue" nations do not really threaten U.S. territory, then a U.S. NMD system cannot really be directed against those threats. Instead, the United States must be seeking to develop a missile defense system that can contribute to its global drive for domination and undermine Russia's nuclear deterrent.

> The results of our military-technical analysis indicate that the threat of the carrying out of a strike against the USA by intercontinental ballistic missiles launched by so-called "problem" states, which the USA sets forth as the primary reason for the development of its national ABM system, is, in reality, not being considered [i.e., it is not the real reason for the

---

[11] Shchedrov, Oleg. Putin sees U.S. missile concerns, but no threat now. Reuters. July 12, 2000.

[12] "The situation indeed has changed, but not enough to break down the system of strategic stability that has formed by emasculating the ABM Treaty. It is possible to take steps to counter the proliferation of missiles and missile technologies without going beyond the framework of the ABM Treaty and by acting above all by means of political and diplomatic methods." See Putin's Nuclear Weapons Reduction Proposals. Moscow, Krasnaya Zvezda, November 14, 2000.

[13] Tretyakov, Vitaliy. The United States is Destroying Strategic Stability. Interview with Russian Federation Defense Minister Marshal Igor Sergeyev. Nezavisimaya Gazeta. June 22, 2000. Translated in FBIS Document CEP20000622000242.

development of the national ABM system]. We do not see any [real] motives for the deployment of this national ABM system other than the striving of the USA to acquire strategic domination in the world. We are deeply convinced that such a deployment would be primarily directed against Russia.[14]

Skepticism About "Limited NMD"

Many Russian officials and analysts do not believe that the United States plans to limit its NMD system. Some argue that the United States would not spend more than $100 billion to develop and deploy a missile defense system, then limit it to a capability to intercept only 10-20 missiles.[15] The Clinton Administration contributed to this disbelief when it stated that it would seek modifications to the ABM Treaty in two phases; the first would simply allow the deployment of a single NMD site in Alaska and the upgrades to some early warning radars. In the second phase, the Clinton Administration planned to request an increase in the permitted number of interceptor missiles and the addition of space-based sensors. Some Russians suspected that additional phases, with additional "minor modifications: would have followed, and that, eventually, the U.S. approach would have loosened the Treaty enough to permit the deployment of more extensive defenses. The Bush Administration also insists that its missile program would be limited to address only the threat from rogue nations. But the Administration has outlined plans to develop and deploy a robust, layered system, as opposed to the limited land-based system considered by the Clinton Administration, which could provide a more capable defense against Russian missiles.

Russian analysts calculated that, even with the Clinton Administration's limited defensive system, the United States could expand its missile defense capabilities by upgrading its early warning and command and control structures, then quickly adding to the number of deployed interceptors. Former Defense Minister Sergeyev outlined this concern in an interview with the Russian press. He noted that "It is not the quantity of interceptor missiles that determines the combat potential of any antimissile defense system. First and foremost, it depends on the system's information components which ensure the acquisition and tracking of targets, the ability

---

[14] Russian Defense Minister Sergeyev on Military Reform, Chechnya, ABM Defense. Vek. February 23, 2001. Translated in FBIS Document Cep20010301000351.

[15] Russian military chief says NMD will destroy strategic stability. Itar-Tass. February 16, 2001. Translated in FBIS Document CEP20010216000210.

to distinguish real warheads from dummy targets."[16] A Russian analyst, Alexander Pikayev, also noted that the United States could easily expand its NMD capabilities once it had developed the space-based sensors that would improve targeting and tracking capabilities. He stated that, once it had developed and deployed these capabilities, "it would be easy for the U.S. to produce and deploy large numbers of interceptors."[17]

In April 2000, Pentagon officials presented Russia's Foreign Minister Igor Ivanov with a detailed briefing about the capabilities of the radars planned for the U.S. NMD system in an effort to convince him that the system would not pose a threat to Russia's strategic deterrent forces.[18] But Russian officials were not convinced.[19] The Bush Administration also provided Russian officials with detailed briefings on the new U.S. missile defense program in early August 2001.

Consequently, with their doubts about the U.S. assessments of emerging ballistic missile threats and their doubts about the limited nature of a prospective U.S. NMD System, many Russian officials and analysts concluded that "the so-called limited nature of the U.S. NMD system is based on the desire to obscure the very essence of the system. The NMD is only a stage in the development and deployment of a full-scale ABM system."[20] Former Defense Minister Sergeyev stated that the Clinton Administration's limited NMD would be the "first step toward the future emergence of a multifunctional global system for combating all types of ballistic, aerodynamic, and space targets and subsequently also surface and land targets. This comprehensive defense system will be directed first and

---

[16] Tretyakov, Vitaliy. The United States is Destroying Strategic Stability. Interview with Russian Federation Defense Minister Marshal Igor Sergeyev. Nezavisimaya Gazeta. June 22, 2000. Translated in FBIS Document CEP20000622000242.

[17] Pikayev, Alexander. ABM Treaty Revision: A Challenge to Russian Security. Disarmament Diplomacy. Issue No. 44.

[18] Myers, Steven Lee. Russians Get Briefing on U.S. Defense Plan. New York Times. April 29, 2000.

[19] "The argument that the US NMD system will be 'limited' in nature and therefore represents no danger to the Russian strategic deterrent forces does not convince us." See, Tretyakov, Vitaliy. The United States is Destroying Strategic Stability. Interview with Russian Federation Defense Minister Marshal Igor Sergeyev. Nezavisimaya Gazeta. June 22, 2000. Translated in FBIS Document CEP20000622000242.

[20] Russian military chief says NMD will destroy strategic stability. Itar-Tass. February 16, 2001. Translated in FBIS Document CEP20010216000210.

foremost against the deterrent potential of the Russian Federation and the People's Republic of China."[21]

The Threat to Russia's Deterrent

Russian analysts have argued that the United States could undermine Russia's strategic nuclear deterrent, and possibly acquire a disarming first strike capability, with even a relatively limited NMD capability. First, they note that Russia's arsenal of strategic offensive nuclear weapons is likely to decline sharply over the next decade, to perhaps fewer than 1,500 warheads, as older weapons are retired and financial constraints preclude the acquisition of newer weapons. But the United States could maintain a much larger offensive nuclear force of several thousand nuclear weapons, even under the terms of the START I and START II Treaties. In addition, NATO enlargement, the U.S. advantage in anti-submarine warfare, and the U.S. advantage in precision-guided conventional weapons, such a the sea-launched Tomahawk cruise missile, provide the United States and its allies with the ability to conduct conventional attacks on strategic targets in Russia in a comprehensive first strike. If the United States launched an attack against Russia with its conventional and nuclear forces, and destroyed a large percentage of Russia's diminished nuclear forces, a few hundred missile defense interceptors could be sufficient to intercept Russia's retaliatory strike. Hence, according to this argument, even a limited NMD system could "undermine strategic stability" and contribute to U.S. efforts to "achieve radical changes in the military balance."[22]

Russian analysts also note that China is likely to react to the deployment of a U.S. NMD system by expanding its military capabilities and its offensive missile forces. One Russian analyst, Alexander Pikayev, has stated that China has already adopted a $10 billion package for a new nuclear buildup in reaction to U.S. plans to deploy an NMD system together with a TMD system in the Western Pacific, and that China would have to significantly increase the size of its missile force to maintain the credibility

---

[21] Tretyakov, Vitaliy. The United States is Destroying Strategic Stability. Interview with Russian Federation Defense Minister Marshall Igor Sergeyev. Nezavisimaya Gazeta. June 22, 2000. Translated in FBIS Document CEP20000622000242.

[22] Rogov, Sergey Mikhaylovich. Reliance on the Nuclear Shield: Not Unilateral Reduction, but a Search for Compromise Solutions With the United States Will Ensure Russia's National Security. August 4, 2000. Translated in FBIS Document

of its deterrent in the face of a U.S. NMD. But, according to Pikayev and other Russian analysts, these weapons could pose as much of a threat to Russia as they could to the United States: "Currently, the predominance of Chinese conventional weapons vis-a-vis the vast but sparsely populated Russian Far East is balanced by Moscow's superiority in nuclear weapons. China's nuclear build-up might considerable erode this superiority, further weakening Russia'' position in the Far East.[23] According to Pikayev, this imbalance with Chinese forces might compel Russia to withdraw from the 1987 Intermediate Forces Treaty.

Possible Military Responses

Hence, in spite of U.S. claims to the contrary, many Russian officials and analysts appear to believe that U.S. withdrawal from the ABM Treaty and deployment of an NMD system would undermine the existing framework of arms control agreements, upset international strategic stability, incite new arms races, and threaten the credibility of Russia's strategic nuclear deterrent. Several Russian officials have declared that, if the United States were to follow this path, Russia would feel compelled to withdraw from a range of arms control agreements so that it could deploy the military forces that it would need to offset the U.S. threat to its nuclear deterrent. These military responses could include changes in the deployment of several different types of nuclear weapons.

Deploy Multiple Warheads on New ICBMs

The 1993 START II Treaty, which has not yet entered into force, would have banned the deployment of land-based strategic ballistic missiles with multiple warheads (MIRVed ICBMs). Under this agreement, Russia would have had to eliminate its 10-warhead SS-18 ICBMs and 10-warhead SS-24 ICBMs. It also would have to reduce, from six to one, the number of warheads deployed on its SS-19 ICBMs. This would leave Russia with an ICBM force that consisted of single warhead SS-25 and SS-27 missiles and around 100 aging SS-19 missiles.

Even without Treaty implementation, Russia is likely to eliminate many of the older multiple warhead missiles. The SS-18s, which have long been

---

CEP20000810000216. See also, Pikayev, Alexander. ABM Treaty Revision: A Challenge to Russian Security. Disarmament Diplomacy. Issue No. 44.

[23] Pikayev, Alexander. ABM Treaty Revision: A Challenge to Russian Security. Disarmament Diplomacy. Issue No. 44.

considered the backbone of Russia's strategic nuclear force, are likely to reach the end of their service-lives by the end of the decade. Russia would find it hard to maintain these forces because the missiles were produced at a plant in Ukraine, which is no longer making ICBMs for Russia, and Russia lacks the economic resources needed to build a new plant to support these missiles in Russia. However, if it were not bound by the START II ban on MIRVed ICBMs, Russia could deploy its older single-warhead SS-25 ICBM and new single-warhead SS-27 ICBM with 3 warheads.[24] Alternatively, Russia could develop new types of decoys and penetration aids for these missiles, to complicate U.S. efforts to intercept them with its missile defense system.

Russia currently has 360 SS-25 missiles and 26 operational SS-27 missiles. The SS-27 missiles were expected to replace the SS-25 missiles in Russia's force. Russia is currently producing fewer than 10 of these missiles per year, but had hoped to produce up to 30 missiles per year later this decade. Many experts believed Russia would eventually produce 300 SS-27 missiles, but with the low production rates currently in place, this number is likely to be lower. Even if each of these missiles were to carry 3 warheads, Russia's ICBM force would likely include fewer than 1000 warheads by the end of the decade. This contrasts with more than 3,500 warheads on Russia's ICBM force now. So, even if Russia were to abrogate START I and set aside START II, it would probably institute sharp reductions in the size of its ICBM force.

Deploy New Intermediate Range Missiles

Several Russian officials have also suggested that Russia might abrogate the 1987 INF Treaty and deploy new shorter-range and intermediate-range missiles.[25] As was noted above, Russia could pursue this option in an effort to offset any advantages that China might acquire if it expanded its nuclear forces in response to a U.S. NMD. But the threat to deploy new missiles in this range can also be seen as a part of Russia" attempt to convince U.S.

---

[24] Dolinin, Aleksandr. Russia's Security Is Reliably Guaranteed. Interview with Strategic Missile Troops Commander-in-Chief, General of the Army Vladimir Yakovlev. Krasnaya Zvezda, July 5, 2000. Translated in FBIS CEP20000705000396.

[25] Dolinin, Aleksandr. Russia's Security Is Reliably Guaranteed. Krasnaya Zvezda, July 5, 2000. Translated in FBIS CEP20000705000396.

allies in Europe to join it in opposing U.S. NMD plans.[26] In discussing this option, Vladimir Yakovlev, the former Commander of Russia's Strategic Rocket Forces noted that "in the event of the repudiation of the INF Treaty, Europe once again falls hostage to a clash between the nuclear superpowers. The United States is planning to [maintain] a 100,000-strong grouping on the continent of Europe with command and control posts and the relevant infrastructure and all this is an extremely worthy target for Russian missiles."[27]

Russia could reportedly produce new intermediate range missiles in a relatively short amount of time. According to one official, the Moscow Institute of Heat and Engineering, Russia's leading design bureau for ballistic missiles, has already prepared blueprints and technical documents for the system and could transfer them to the Votkinsk missile assembly facility as soon as a decision was made to begin producing missiles.[28] Nevertheless, it is unlikely that it could produce large numbers of these missiles in a short period of time. The Votkinsk Missile Assembly facility is the same location where Russia produced the SS-25 missiles and is currently producing the SS-27 missile, at a rate of fewer than 10 per year. Economic constraints would make it very difficult for Russia to expand production at this facility. Hence, any increase in the production of intermediate-range missiles could come at the expense of the already-low production rate for SS-27 missiles.

Redeploy Shorter-range Nuclear Delivery Systems

During the early 1990s, the United States and Soviet Union both withdrew from deployment many of their shorter-range nuclear delivery systems. They did this unilaterally, without any negotiated agreements and without any formal monitoring or verification provisions. For Russia, these weapons came out of deployment areas in the other former Soviet republics and near Russia's borders. Many were consolidated at storage areas within Russia. Some analysts in the United States have expressed concerns that Russia might return some of these weapons to deployment or to storage areas closer to Russia's western borders. The Commander of Russia's Strategic

---

[26] Saradzhyan, Simon. U.S. NMD Effort Fueling Russia's New Missile Plan. Defense News. July 10, 2000, p. 1.

[27] Odnokolenko, Oleg. Wait For a Response. Asymmetrical Response. Russia Could Be Embroiled in Ruinous Arms Race. Segodnya, June 22, 2000. Translated in FBIS Document CEP20000622000085.

[28] Saradzhyan, Simon. U.S. NMD Effort Fueling Russia's New Missile Plan. Defense News. July 10, 2000. p. 1.

Rocket forces indicated that this was a possibility when he stated that Russia could also institute "changes to the principles of employment and deployment of operational-tactical nuclear weapons" as a part of its response to U.S. deployment of NMD.[29]

This type of response would not give Russia any new capabilities to threaten the United States or to penetrate U.S. missile defenses. However, it would be consistent with Russia's new national security strategy, which allows for the possible use of non-strategic nuclear weapons in response to conventional military attacks on Russia. Most experts believe that this change in Russia's strategy is a response to the degradation in Russia's conventional military capabilities, and its growing concern about the military implications of NATO enlargement. In addition, the threat of new nuclear deployments near Europe could be a part of Russia's efforts to draw support from the United States' allies in Europe for Russia's opposition to missile defense. According to this school of thought, the more threatened the Europeans feel by Russia's potential responses, the more likely they are to pressure the United States to alter its policy on missile defense.

Most experts agree that Russia will not be able to win the support of U.S. allies in Europe, even if it threatens to redeploy shorter-range or intermediate-range nuclear forces near its western borders. However, if Russia intends to make these changes anyway, in response to its diminished conventional capabilities, then the collapse of arms control in response to U.S. missile defense policy could provide a convenient excuse.

RUSSIAN ALTERNATIVES

Russian officials have stated that, instead of relying on missile defenses that could upset stability and undermine arms control, the two sides should rely on "an umbrella based on diplomacy"[30] and has offered proposals for measures that the international community might adopt to address the threat posed by missile proliferation. The Clinton Administration did not dismiss the Russian approach, but also did not accept it as an alternative to the U.S.

---

[29] Dolinin, Aleksandr. Russia's Security Is Reliably Guaranteed. Interview with Strategic Missile Troops Commander-in-Chief, General of the Army Vladimir Yakovlev. Krasnaya Zvezda, July 5, 2000. Translated in FBIS CEP20000705000396.

[30] Williams, Daniel. Russia Wants Political Shield; Moscow Says Diplomacy, Not Technology, Key to Missile Defense. Washington Post. June 14, 2000. p. A34.

approach. Then-Secretary of Defense Cohen noted, after the June 2000 summit between Presidents Clinton and Putin, that the response to missile proliferation should include both diplomatic efforts to stop proliferation and defensive systems to protect the nations from possible attack.[31]

The Global Missile and Missile Technology Non-Proliferation Control System (GCS)

In June 1999, Russia proposed that the international community establish a Global Missile and Missile Technology Non-proliferation Control System (GCS). Russia advocated this regime as "component part of the global regime of the non-proliferation of missiles and missile technologies."[32] It would, in part, complement the Missile Technology Control Regime – which regulates the supply side of missile technologies – by regulating the behavior of nations that might seek to acquire ballistic missile technologies; and, would operate under U.N. auspices. It would also provide incentives to nations so that they would forgo their own missile arsenals. Russian officials said the goal was to present an alternative to NMD that maximizes "peaceful" diplomatic and political efforts to address concerns about missile proliferation.[33]

Specifically, Russia proposed that the international community create a pre-launch and post-launch notification launch-monitoring regime to build transparency into ballistic missile developments. Nations that participated in this regime would gain an understanding of missile developments in neighboring countries and might feel less threatened, and therefore, less compelled to develop their own missiles. The regime would also include a global monitoring system to provide a "mechanism for detection of missile launches for any purpose." This monitoring system, which could build on the system under development by the United States and Russia, might also ease tensions and uncertainties about ballistic missile developments. For nations who agreed to forgo the development of their own ballistic missiles, the Russian proposal offered security guarantees, with the international community coming to a nation's assistance if it were attacked by ballistic

---

[31] DOD News Briefing, Secretary of Defense William S. Cohen, Presenter. June 9, 2000.
[32] Ivanov Comments on START-3 Negotiations, Moscow Ministry of Foreign Affairs of the Russian Federation, September 2, 2000. Translated in FBIS Document CEP20000905000219.
[33] U.S. Adopting "Wait and See" Approach to Russian Missile Initiative. Inside the Pentagon, April 16, 2000. p. 1.

missiles. Finally, the proposal contained incentives for countries to forgo the development of ballistic missiles.[34]

The Clinton Administration responded cautiously to the Russian proposal. It reportedly saw some positive elements, but also had concerns that the discussions might be used as a forum to criticize U.S. NMD plans and undermine U.S. efforts to win support for missile defenses.[35] Furthermore, although the United States supported the principle of a multilateral launch notification regime, it preferred to focus its attention on the bilateral U.S.-Russian effort. It believed it would be easier to make the Joint Data Exchange Center available to other countries once it was operational than to conduct multilateral negotiations to establish the center.

Russia has held two organization meetings on its proposal for a GCS. At the first conference, in March 2000, Russia outlined its plan for the regime. At the second, in February 2001, the participants talked about an international code of conduct on missile technology transfers that had been proposed at the MTCR meetings last year. This code would affect the demand side, placing limits on nations seeking to advance their missile capabilities. The United States has not participated actively in the GCS forum. The U.S. embassy sent an observer to the first meeting but no U.S. official attended the second. The Clinton Administration agreed to try to integrate the GCS proposal into the existing MTCR framework, but it did not support the creation of a separate regime outside of the MTCR framework.[36]

Cooperation on Theater Ballistic Missile Defenses in Europe

The Russian Proposal

Russia's President Vladimir Putin first proposed that Russia cooperate with nations in Europe in developing defenses against theater ballistic missiles in June 2000, shortly after his summit meeting with President Clinton. He referred to this concept as "a regionally-based missile defense system" that would not require any changes in the ABM Treaty.[37] Putin's initial, general proposal was followed by meetings between NATO officials

---

[34] U.S. Adopting "Wait and See" Approach to Russian Missile Initiative. Inside the Pentagon, April 16, 2000. p. 1.
[35] U.S. Adopting "Wait and See" Approach to Russian Missile Initiative. Inside the Pentagon, April 16, 2000. p. 1.
[36] Russia Holds Second GCS Conference. Arms Control Today. March 2001. p. 34.
[37] Europe Urged by Putin to Reject U.S. Missile Plan. London Times, June 12, 2000.

and Russia's Minister of Defense, Igor Sergeyev, later in June. At that time, General Sergeyev reportedly outlined the framework for cooperation that Russia had in mind. He said that possible areas of cooperation could include:

- joint assessment of the nature and scale of missile proliferation and possible missile threats;

- joint development of a concept for a pan-European nonstrategic missile defense system and of a procedure for its creation and deployment;

- joint creation of a pan-European multilateral missile launch warning center;

- the holding of joint command and staff exercises;
- the conducting of joint research and experiments;

- joint development of nonstrategic missile defense systems;

- creation of nonstrategic missile defense formations for joint or coordinated actions to protect peacekeeping forces or the civilian population.[38]

Russia's second proposal was included in a nine-page paper entitled "Phases of European Missile Defense" that was presented to NATO's Secretary General Lord George Robertson in Moscow in February 2001. This paper reportedly added details to the general outline that Russia had first presented in June 2000. One key difference was that, instead of hinting at the use of boost-phase defenses, as Russia had done in June 2000, the new paper indicated that the defensive system would rely on more conventional terminal defenses in transportable units that could be moved to counter specific threats during a crisis.[39] But the rest of the proposal remained essentially the same. Russia and the European nations would first cooperate in a forum that would review and assess emerging ballistic missile threats. They could then establish a joint early warning center to process data and share information on missile launches. These nations could also jointly

---

[38] Tretyakov, Vitaliy. The United States is Destroying Strategic Stability. Interview with Russian Federation Defense Minister Marshal Igor Sergeyev. Nezavisimaya Gazeta. June 22, 2000. Translated in FBIS Document CEP20000633000242.
[39] Baker, Peter and Susan B. Glasser. Russia Details Anti-Missile Alternative. Washington Post. February 21, 2001. p. 16.

develop, build and deploy a non-strategic anti-ballistic missile system that could be ready for rapid deployment to any area in Europe where the threat of missile attack might arise.[40] According to some reports, the plan was "long on generalities and short on specifics." It provided "little technical evaluation and no cost estimates, development timetables, or organizational structures." It simply represented a "theoretical basis for how a mobile European-based system might be developed using Russian technology."[41]

Russian officials emphasized that Russia had the technology, industrial base, and testing facilities needed to develop and produce a mobile non-strategic ballistic missile defense system. They also noted that Russia had the early warning network needed to monitor and respond to ballistic missile threats that might emerge from nations to the south of Europe.[42] The paper presented to Lord Robertson did not identify the technologies that could be used in the system, but it did contain a diagram, and analysts who reviewed the material concluded that Russia intended to use its S-300 and S-400 air-defense systems.[43] The S-300 reportedly includes a sophisticated set of tracking devices and rockets that can reportedly intercept up to six missiles or aircraft at one time.[44] These systems are reportedly based on the SA-10 air-defense system that the Soviet Union first deployed in the late 1960s. The system accomplished some successful intercepts of theater-range ballistic missiles in the mid-1990s. Jane's Strategic Weapons Systems attributes this system with capabilities similar to the U.S. Patriot system, which can intercept shorter-range ballistic missiles.[45] But Russian sources claim the S-400 version will be able to intercept missiles with ranges up to 3,500 kilometers. This version reportedly entered production in mid-2000 and may become operational in 2001.[46]

---

[40] Russia Sees Rapid Anti-Missile Force. New York Times on the Web. April 10, 2001.
[41] Baker, Peter. Russia's Skeletal Missile Plan. Outline of European Shield Brings Little Response from the West. Washington Post. April 3, 2001.
[42] Sorokina, Svetlana. Interview with Vladimir Yakovlev, Commander in Chief of the Russian Strategic Missile Troops. From the "Hero of the Day" program, June 22, 2000. Translated in FBIS Document CEP20000622000323.
[43] Baker, Peter. Russia's Skeletal Missile Plan. Outline of European Shield Brings Little Response from the West. Washington Post. April 3, 2001.
[44] Hoagland, Jim. Putin's Rocket Challenge. Washington Post. March 18, 2001. p. B7.
[45] Lennox, Duncan, editor. Jane's Strategic Weapons Systems. Issue 33. August 2000. pp. 302-305.
[46] Missile Troops Begin Testing of S-400 Defensive Missile System. Moscow TV. June 21, 2000.

The U.S. and European Reactions

When Russia first offered its proposal for a European missile defense system, the Clinton Administration said the idea could not serve as a substitute for a U.S. NMD. Specifically, Secretary of Defense Cohen stated that it would leave the United States and Europe vulnerable to attacks from long-range rockets being developed by countries such as Iran and North Korea. Therefore, it could not protect the United States or its allies from the full range of emerging threats.[47] To be acceptable to the United States, a missile defense system would have to "protect all of the United States territory." Therefore, the Russian suggestion for a cooperative system with Europe "could supplement, but not substitute for the system that the U.S. is developing."[48]

The European reaction to Russia's initial proposal was also "guarded." According to a European diplomat, "There is a lot of skepticism because this would seem to be another attempt by Moscow to drive a wedge between Europe and the United States."[49] Many analysts also considered the proposal to be a "clumsy" attempt by Moscow to draw the European nations away from the United States and to increase pressure on the Clinton Administration to defer missile defense deployment and remain within the ABM Treaty.

The reaction to Russia's February 2001 paper that added details to the June 2000 proposal was not as critical. Officials from both the Bush Administration and NATO noted that Russia's focus on theater missile defenses for Europe indicated that Russia appeared to agree with the United States that missile proliferation posed a threat and agreed that missile defense systems, as well as diplomacy and arms control, could play a role in addressing the threat.[50] Some analysts suggested that a change in tone that accompanied Russia's second proposal, and the fact that it came less than a month into the Bush Administration, signaled that Russia realized that the new President was more committed to the deployment of missile defenses and that Russia's opposition could be futile. Instead, by offering more details

---

[47] Drozdiak, William. U.S. Rejects Russian Plan for Joint Missile Defense. Cohen Says Proposal Fails to Shield Against Long-Range Strikes. Washington Post. June 10, 2000, p. 17.

[48] DOD News Briefing. Secretary of Defense William S. Cohen, Presenter. June 9, 2000.

[49] Drozdiak, William. U.S. Rejects Russian Plan for Joint Missile Defense. Cohen Says Proposal Fails to Shield Against Long-Range Strikes. Washington Post. June 10, 2000, p. 17.

[50] Gordon, Michael R. Moscow Signaling A Change in Tone on Missile Defense. New York Times, February 22, 2001. p. 1.

on the Russian alternative, Russia could be seeking to maintain a dialogue with the United States on missile defenses.[51]

U.S. RESPONSES TO THE RUSSIAN REACTION

Clinton Administration

The Clinton Administration sought to address Russian concerns about the U.S. plans for missile defense by convincing Russia that the ABM Treaty would remain largely in place, that missile defenses would remain relatively limited, and that they would be directed against possible small-scale attacks from "rogue" nations. As was noted above, the Clinton Administration agreed with the Russian view that the ABM Treaty was the cornerstone of strategic stability. It proposed only modest changes to the Treaty, so that it could deploy a limited ground-based site in Alaska, rather than North Dakota, and so that it could upgrade radar capabilities. It acknowledged that the United States might seek further modifications in the future, but it never suggested that it would deploy a robust, layered defense that included sea-based or space-based interceptors.

Administration officials also met frequently with Russian officials to discuss U.S. NMD plans and to seek Russian agreement on changes to the ABM Treaty. Although these discussions proved futile, and Russia offered little more than a simple "no" in response to U.S. initiatives, this effort appeared to indicate that the United States placed a high priority on reaching agreement with Russia before it proceeded with its missile defense plans. Administration officials indicated that the United states would consider withdrawing from the ABM Treaty if Russia failed to accept modifications but Russia apparently never believed that the Clinton Administration would take this step. This view may have contributed to Russia's reluctance to accept or even discuss the U.S. proposals.

Bush Administration

---

[51] Gordon, Michael R. Moscow Signaling Signaling A Change in Tone on Missile Defense. New York Times, February 22, 2001. p. 1.

The Bush Administration has altered sharply the U.S. approach towards addressing Russia's concerns. First, the Administration does not support the view that the ABM Treaty remains the cornerstone of strategic stability. To the contrary, Secretaries Rumsfeld and Powell have stated that the Treaty is "ancient history" and "not relevant in the current strategic framework." In his speech on May 1, 2001, President Bush said the United States must "leave behind the constraints of the ABM Treaty" and, instead, "replace this treaty with a new framework that reflects a clear and clean break from the past...."

Second, the Bush Administration has not accepted the limited approach to missile defenses that had been pursued by the Clinton Administration. Although the Administration insists that its defensive systems will also be directed against "rogue" nation threats and accidental launches, it has not pledged to keep that system limited to a few hundred interceptors based at one or a few sites on land. Instead, the Administration has pledged to develop a "layered" defense that will include components based on land, at sea, and in space. Unlike the Clinton Administration, and possibly because it has not yet settled on an architecture, the Bush Administration has not yet sought to convince Russia that the technologies included in U.S. missile defense plans could not intercept a deliberate Russian attack and would not undermine Russia's deterrent. Instead, the Administration has offered verbal assurances that it does not view Russia as an adversary, and, therefore, would not direct U.S. missile defense efforts against Russian forces.

In late July 2001, Presidents Bush and Putin agreed that the two nations would hold discussions on their offensive nuclear weapons and missile defenses, and seek to reach agreement on a new strategic framework. These discussions began in early August, when Russian officials received a detailed briefing on U.S. technologies and the Bush Administration plans for missile defenses. But the Bush Administration does not view these discussions as the opening round in a formal negotiating process that might produce a new treaty limiting offensive nuclear weapons or missile defenses. The President and officials in his Administration have argued that, in the absence of an adversarial relationship between the two nations, formal arms control agreements are no longer needed to manage their relationship. Instead, the United States may be seeking a more informal process where the two sides simply inform each other of their plans and programs. In addition, the United States would like Russia to agree to set aside the ABM Treaty, or to have both parties withdraw from it together, so that the United States can proceed with missile defense. President Bush has also stated that, if the two sides could not soon reach an agreement to set the Treaty aside together, the

United States would withdraw and deploy defenses. In addition, Secretary Powell has announced that the United States wold no longer participate in the Standing Consultative Commission (SCC), where the parties to the ABM Treaty discuss implementation and compliance issues.[52]

Russia, on the other hand, would probably prefer to keep some form of Treaty regime in place. It acknowledges that the world has changed and that the relationship with the United States has changed, but it continues to place a value on the predictability and formality offered by arms control agreements. Reports indicate that it may be willing to permit more extensive testing of missile defense systems, and to relax the definitions in the Agreed Statements on Demarcation so that the United States can test TMD systems against a wider range of targets. But, even if it may now e willing to modify the ABM Treaty so that the United States can conduct these tests, it does not favor an environment in which the United States can deploy defenses without limits.

Many experts believe that Russia is willing to engage in discussions with the Bush Administration because Russian officials believe that the Administration is so committed to missile defenses that it would be willing, if not eager, to withdraw from the ABM Treaty. This view seemed evident in Russia's initial reaction to president Bush's speech on missile defense policy. Foreign Minister Ivanov, in a press conference after the speech, praised the President's call for discussions about strategic stability and a new strategic framework. However, he did not appear to accept the Administration's view that this new framework could replace the ABM Treaty. He said that Russia would "insist on preserving and strengthening" the ABM Treaty and that the Treaty cannot be separated "from the general architecture" of arms control agreements "that has been formed in the last 30 years and that has become the basis of international security."[53]

Hence, although the Bush Administration appears to place a lower priority on reaching agreement with the Russians than did the Clinton Administration, it also appears that the Russians may be less resistant to reaching an agreement now that it believes the United States is more likely to withdraw from the ABM Treaty. However, it remains to be seen whether Russia will alter its positions on the dangers of missile defense for Russia's

---

[52] Pincus, Walter. U.S. Considers Shift in Nuclear Targets. Defenses to Focus on China, Expert Says. Washington Post. April 29, 2001. p.23.
[53] Tyler, Patrick E. Global Reaction to Missile Plan is Cautious. New York Times, May 3, 2001.

nuclear deterrent and importance of the ABM Treaty for international strategic stability.

Issues for Congress

Members of Congress have expressed a range of opinions about the Bush Administration's approach to missile defense and arms control.[54] Congress is not likely to vote directly on binding legislation that would address the question of whether the United States should withdraw from the ABM Treaty. It will, however, have annual opportunities to review the Administration's plans for missile defenses, and their implications for the ABM Treaty when it reviews the Administration's budget requests during the annual authorization and appropriations process. These debates may be dominated by questions about the costs and technical feasibility of U.S. missile defense plans. But the Members may also address some questions about the implications of these plans for the U.S. relationship with Russia and the future of the arms control process.

Will Russia Continue to Cooperate on Offensive Arms Reductions?

Many critics of U.S. missile defense policy consider Russia's threat to withdraw from a range of offensive arms control agreements as a key threat to U.S. security. They note that these agreements not only reduce the size of the only arsenal that can threaten U.S. survival, but they also include monitoring and verification provisions that bring predictability, transparency, and cooperation to the U.S.-Russian nuclear relationship. Others, however, argue that the benefits of arms control are not worth the cost of remaining vulnerable to missile attack. They note that Russian nuclear forces are likely to decline sharply during the next decade under economic constraints, with or without arms control. They also note that the United States could reduce its offensive forces, as President Bush has promised to do, without negotiating formal agreements. Finally, they contend that the United States and Russia have established a mature, cooperative relationship on nuclear weapons issues and that the transparency

---

[54] See, for example, Biden, Joseph R., Jr. Missile Defense Will Make Us Less Secure, Wall Street Journal, May 3, 2001; John Kyl. ABM Treaty Must Go. USA Today, May 2, 2001. p. 12; and Alison Mitchell, Senate Democrats Square Off with Bush Over Missile Plan. New York Times, May 3, 2001. p. 1.

and predictability from this relationship could continue even if the countries were not monitoring compliance with arms control treaties.

Will Russia Continue to Cooperate in Non-proliferation and Threat Reduction Activities?

Some critics of U.S. missile defense policy argue that Russia might cease its cooperation in a range of other policy areas if the United States were to withdraw from the ABM Treaty. They point to Russia's expanding nuclear cooperation with Iran as evidence that Russia could do serious harm to U.S. national security if it chose to pursue a less restrained non-proliferation policy. Some also contend that Russia might withdraw from participation in the Nunn-Lugar Cooperative Threat Reduction Program, where the United States provides financial and technical assistance in securing and eliminating Russian nuclear weapons and materials. Without U.S. participation, these weapons and materials might be lost, stolen, or sold to nations seeking their own nuclear weapons. Some believe these possibilities could pose a greater threat to U.S. security than the emerging missile threats that would be the target of U.S. missile defenses.

Others, however, doubt that Russian policies in these areas would be linked to U.S. withdrawal from the ABM Treaty. They note that Russia has been cooperating with Iran in nuclear developments and military sales for many years, and that these activities are driven more by Russia's interest in earning hard currency than by Russia's interest in undermining U.S. non-proliferation objectives. Some also argue that Russia would not be likely to cut off cooperation under the Nunn-Lugar programs because it recognizes the threats posed by the potential loss of nuclear weapons and materials and it would be unable to safeguard and eliminate aging nuclear weapons without U.S. assistance.

Will Russia Convince Other Nations to Support its Objections to U.S. Missile Defense Policies?

Russia has been conducting a world-wide public relations campaign in an effort to win the support of other countries in its opposition to U.S. missile defense policies. It has joined with China on numerous occasions to criticize U.S. missile defenses as a threat to international stability and it has sought to win support from U.S. allies in Europe by promising to cooperate on the development of theater missile defenses for Europe. It has also issued declarations with many other nations in support of the ABM Treaty and opposition to U.S. missile defense plans.

Some critics of U.S. missile defense plans argue that the United States might find itself isolated in the international community if it continues to pursue missile defenses and withdraws from the ABM Treaty. They note that most countries are at least uncomfortable, if not outright opposed. to this policy. Some fear that these nations might interfere with or complicate other areas of U.S. policy if they feel that the United States has upset the international order with its pursuit of missile defenses.

The Bush Administration has pledged to consult with U.S. allies before it proceeds with missile defense, in part to ease their concerns and reduce their resistance. Supporters of missile defense deployments generally support consultation with U.S. allies, although some have expressed concern that the Administration's emphasis on these consultations could leave U.S. policy vulnerable to the objections of other nations. And many do not think these objections will affect the U.S. international position. They argue that U.S. missile defenses will enhance, not degrade, international security, and that other nations will realize that they will benefit in the long run if the United States pursues this course. Some also note that international criticism will not, in the long run, affect U.S. policy objectives.

CONCLUSION

It is not clear, at this time, whether Russia will continue to press its objections to U.S. policies on missile defense and the ABM Treaty, or whether it will try to reach an accommodation with the Bush Administration on a new framework for strategic stability. Many members of the Bush Administration seem to believe that the United States will gain Russia's cooperation when Russia realizes that the U.S. is prepared to withdraw from the ABM Treaty. They note that Russia remains extremely interested in reductions in offensive nuclear forces and that the Bush Administration's plans to reduce U.S. forces will ease Russia's concerns about U.S. intentions. Eventually, they believe that Russia will cooperate with the United States in a transition to a new strategic framework that combines both offensive and defensive weapons in the deterrence equation.

Others, however, argue that Russia has outlined well-reasoned and complex objections to U.S. policy on missile defense and the ABM Treaty, and that it is not likely to change its views in the near term. Instead, they believe that, if and when the United States withdraws from the ABM Treaty,

Russia could follow through on its threats to withdraw from a range of arms control agreements and its plans to augment its nuclear forces. They argue that the United States might eventually become less secure than it is today, even if it deploys missile defenses, because it will be faced with a more adversarial, less cooperative Russia. And Russia will retain enough nuclear weapons to saturate the U.S. defenses and threaten the survival of the United States.

INDEX

A

ABM interceptor missile(s), 9, 11, 12, 78, 102
ABM mode, 9-12, 14, 15, 50
ABM radar, 11-15
ABM system(s), 9, 10, 12-14, 78, 79, 102, 103, 105, 108, 110
ABM Treaty, 2, 3, 5, 6, 8-11, 13-20, 25, 38-41, 50, 70, 71, 75-79, 81-84, 86, 87, 90-94, 99-106, 108-112, 117, 120-126
accountability, 34
acquisition strategy, 1, 27, 30, 32, 34
Aegis Spy-1 radar, 11, 15, 16, 53
Aegis, 11, 14-16, 43, 44, 53-58, 66, 85
Afghanistan, 26, 41
Agreed Statements on Demarcation, 12, 19, 122
air defense capability, 20
Air Force Airborne Laser (ABL), 21, 47, 48, 49
Air Force Space Based Laser Experiment, 21
Air Force, 12, 15, 20, 21, 31, 47, 67, 70
Air-Based Boost, 21, 47
Alaska, 5, 11-14, 16, 37, 38, 53, 54, 57, 84, 88, 89, 91, 94, 95, 103, 109, 121
Aldridge, Edward C. "Pete", 64
AMB systems, 78, 79
American Missile protection Act of 1998, 96
anti-ballistic missile (ABM) systems, 79
anti-missile defense, 43
Armitage, Richard L., 45
arms control agreements, 18, 19, 38, 41, 89, 99, 100, 112, 122-124, 126
arms control treaties, 92, 124
arms control, 3, 14, 17-19, 38-41, 76, 82, 87, 89, 92, 93, 99-101, 105, 112, 115, 120, 122-124, 126
arms race, 38, 99, 106
Army, 2, 10, 12, 13, 20, 26, 59-61, 63, 65, 70, 72, 112, 114
Arrow Deployability Program (ADP), 21
ASEAN Regional Forum, 45
Aspin, Les, 80
Australia, 41, 44, 45

B

ballistic missile attack(s), 4, 6, 9, 10, 32, 53, 78, 84, 102, 104
ballistic missile defense (BMD), 2, 6, 21, 24, 33, 35, 37, 42, 44, 45, 55, 58, 69-71, 73, 75, 77, 80, 87, 106, 118
Ballistic Missile Defense Organization (BMDO), 2, 6, 14, 15, 16, 20, 21, 24, 32, 34, 36, 37, 47, 48, 51-55, 58, 60-62, 66, 69, 70, 81, 89, 90, 95
ballistic missile proliferation, 84, 107
ballistic missiles, 5, 9, 13, 27, 28, 42, 43, 46, 49-51, 54, 57, 58, 61, 75, 76, 77, 80, 86, 87, 99-101, 108, 112, 113, 116, 117, 119
Battle Management, Command, Control, and Communications (BMC$^{3)}$, 53
Battle Management, Command, Control, and Communications, 53, 81
Beale Air Force Base, 12
Belarus, 18, 102
Bharatiya Janata Party (BJP), 45
Biden, Senator, 82
bilateral treaty, 17
Biological Weapons Protocol, 40
biological weapons, 89
Blair, Prime Minister Tony, 40
BMD technology, 21, 42
Boeing, 47, 48, 50, 53, 54, 68, 81, 84
Bolton, John, 8, 19
Boost Phase Segment, 70
Britain, 40
budget requests, 36, 123
budgetary analysis, 21
Bush Administration, vii, 1-4, 6-8, 10, 11, 14, 18, 20, 21, 39, 40, 42-46, 50, 53, 60, 62, 66, 76, 80, 83, 84, 87, 93, 95, 100, 103, 104, 109, 110, 120-123, 125, 126

Bush, President, 6, 8, 17, 19, 40, 76, 77, 93, 103, 104, 121, 122, 124

C

C^3I system, 37
Carter Administration, 79
China, vii, 2, 4, 5, 41, 42, 43, 46, 89, 92, 93, 106, 110, 111, 113, 122, 125
Chirac, President Jacques, 40
Clinton Administration, 3, 5, 6, 7, 12, 13, 18, 38, 46, 53, 62, 75, 76, 78, 80, 81, 82, 83, 86, 87, 88, 91, 94, 95, 99, 100, 101, 102, 103, 106, 109, 110, 115, 116, 117, 119, 120, 121, 123
Cobra Dane radar, 12
Cold War, 83, 105, 108
Compliance Review Group (CRG), 16
compliance, 2, 11, 13, 15, 38, 96, 122, 124
Comprehensive Test Ban Treaty (CTBT), 46
Comptroller General, 35
conference report, 35, 37, 60
Congressional Budget Office (CBO), 68, 94
congressional oversight, 24, 31
conventional military forces, 2
countermeasures, 7, 30, 48, 60, 61
counterterrorism, 25, 69
cryocooler, 68
cyberwarfare, 25

D

Defense Acquisition Board (DAB), 62
Defense Authorization Bill, 11, 16, 82, 85, 96
defense budget, 4, 6, 21, 26, 27, 35, 44, 65, 96

Index

Defense Minister Ivanov, 39
defense spending, 3, 24, 26, 72
Department of Defense (DoD), 2, 4, 13, 16, 24-27, 30, 31, 32, 34-36, 44, 48, 51, 54, 56- 58, 60, 61, 64-71, 80, 89-91, 95, 107, 115, 120
Deployment Readiness Review (DRR), 87, 90
deployment, 1-10, 24, 31-33, 37, 38, 48, 59, 63, 69, 75-87, 89-93, 95-97, 99-103, 105-112, 114, 117, 118, 120
Desert Storm, 28
deterrence, 1, 32, 40, 84, 104, 105, 108, 126
diplomacy, 101, 115, 120

E

early missile defense system, 37
engineering and manufacturing development (EMD), 36, 48, 61, 68, 72
Environmental Impact Statement (EIS), 95
Europe, 39, 40, 76, 86, 93, 100, 113-115, 117-120, 125
European Union (EU), 40, 41
evolutionary acquisition, 7, 30, 31, 32, 34, 37

F

Flight Demonstration System (FDS), 67
France, 40, 64
Ft. Greely, 11, 12, 15, 37, 53
funding, 1, 3, 4, 6, 10, 21, 22, 24-26, 32, 35, 36, 44, 47, 50, 52, 57-60, 62, 63, 66, 67-70, 72, 76, 78, 81, 82, 96
Future Years Defense Plan (FYDP), 27, 35, 68, 78, 80, 81, 95

FY2002 defense authorization bill, 16, 24, 25, 35, 52, 57, 60, 63, 69, 70
FY2003 Defense Authorization Bill, 2, 73

G

Gates Commission, 88
General Accounting Office (GAO), 60, 68, 94
Germany, 40, 60, 63
Global Missile and Missile Technology Non-proliferation Control System (GCS), 115, 117
Global Protection Against Limited Strikes (GPALS), 79, 80
Ground-Based Interceptor, 81
Ground-Based Midcourse, 21, 53, 55
Ground-Based Terminal, 21, 59
Gulf War, 59

H

Hawaii, 88, 89
HAWK air defense system, 62
Heritage Foundation, 85
hit-to-kill, 27, 57, 59, 61, 62, 90
homeland defense, 25
House Appropriations Committee, 36, 59, 68, 69, 71
House Armed Services Committee (HAS), 2, 52, 57, 60, 63, 66, 69, 73, 97
Howard, Prime Minister John, 44

I

ICBMs, 30, 41, 44, 89, 100, 108, 112
Improved 8-Pack missile, 56
India, 41, 45, 46
Initial Operational Capability (IOC), 53

Integrated Flight Test (IFT), 15, 54
intelligence community, 88, 89
intercept(or) tests, 15, 25, 27, 55, 58
interceptors, 7, 10, 12-14, 27, 37, 50, 51, 53, 58, 75, 76, 79, 81, 82, 85, 91, 94, 95, 103, 109, 111, 121
intermediate-range missiles, 100, 113, 114
Intermediate-Range Nuclear Forces (INF), 38, 113
international community, 92, 100, 101, 107, 115, 116, 125
international law, 17
international security, 83, 92, 107, 123, 125
Iran, 40, 52, 88, 89, 100, 119, 124, 125
Iraq, 40, 77, 89, 100
Iraqi Scud missiles, 27
Israel, 60
Israeli Arrow Deployability program, 21
Italy, 8, 18, 40, 60, 63

J

Japan, 41, 42, 43, 44, 60
Japanese government, 42
joint assessment, 117
Joint Data Exchange Center, 116
Joint Statement on Principles of Strategic Stability, 106, 107

K

Kadish, General, 6, 51, 56, 68
Kadish, Lt. Gen. Ronald, 32
Kadish, Ronald, 67
Kazakhstan, 18, 102
kinetic energy, 49, 51, 61
kinetic kill vehicle (KKV), 54, 56, 57, 65
kinetic kill, 27, 28, 53
Kodiak Island, 12

Kwajalein Missile Range, 14, 15

L

layered defense(s), 7, 10, 20, 28-30, 32, 84, 121
Lead System Integrator (LSI), 53
Levin, Senator, 16, 70, 77
Libya, 52
life cycle costs, 47, 59, 61
Lightweight Exo-Atmospheric Projectile (LEAP), 55-57
Lockheed Martin, 48, 50, 54, 61, 63, 65, 68
long-range missiles, 7, 24, 28, 43, 88, 108
Lott, Senator Trent, 83

M

Medium Extended Air Defense System (MEADS), 20, 21, 60-64, 69-71
medium-range missiles, 24, 55, 59
Memorandum of Understanding (MOUS), 18, 63, 102
Memorandum of Understanding on Succession, 18, 102
Middle East, 61
military balance, 111
military capabilities, 3, 42, 100, 106, 111, 114
Missile Defense Agency (MDA), 2, 6, 20, 24, 32, 35, 47, 48, 51, 52, 66-69, 72, 73
missile defense budget, 6
missile defense program, 1, 4, 6, 7, 10, 12, 20, 21, 26, 27, 36, 41, 50, 58, 71, 104, 110
missile defense technologies, 7, 10, 83
missile defense test, 11
Missile Technology Control Regime, 116

missile threats, 5, 40, 60, 78, 85, 87, 94, 101, 107, 108, 110, 117, 118, 119, 125
multilateral treaty, 17
multiple independent reentry vehicles (MIRVs), 42
multiple missile defenses, 20
Munich Conference, 84

N

National Missile Defense (NMD) system, 75, 76, 80-82, 85, 89, 91-96, 99, 101, 103, 107, 110, 111
national missile defense (NMD), 5, 6, 13, 21, 24, 37, 43, 45, 53, 54, 56, 57, 75-97, 99-101, 103-114, 116, 119, 121
national security, 4, 39, 64, 82, 90, 92, 114, 124
national territory, 9, 78, 102
NATO, 41, 62, 63, 77, 84, 93, 111, 114, 117, 118, 120
Naval Surface Warfare Center (NSCWC), 65
Navy Area Defense (NAD), 21, 64-66, 69
Navy Theater-Wide (NTW), 21, 43, 44, 54-57, 62
Navy Upper Tier program, 54
Navy, 15, 20, 21, 26, 43, 51, 52, 54, 56-59, 65, 66, 69, 70, 76, 85
Netherlands, 60, 64
Nixon Administration, 79
non-ABM radars, 14
non-nuclear ballistic missile defenses, 79
nonproliferation policy, 46, 82
non-proliferation, 40, 46, 115, 124, 125
North Dakota, 10, 75, 79, 95, 121
North Korea, vii, 43, 44, 52, 77, 88, 89, 100, 119

nuclear balance, 101
nuclear stability, 5
nuclear weapons, 2, 8, 18, 27, 38, 46, 96, 100, 105, 110, 111, 112, 114, 122, 124-126
Nunn-Lugar Cooperative Threat Reduction Program, 124
Nunn-McCurdy provision, 64

O

Office of Test and Evaluation, 48

P

PAC-3, 2, 14, 27, 28, 59, 60, 63, 65, 69, 70, 72, 73
Pakistan, 46
Patriot Advanced Capability-3, 59
Patriot PAC-3, 14, 20, 21, 59, 61, 62, 63
Pentagon, 2, 14, 15, 16, 18, 24-26, 37, 51, 60-65, 71, 72, 90, 94, 104, 110, 116
Pentagon's Operational Test & Evaluation directorate, 90
People's Republic of China (PRC), 41
performance goals, 35
Persian Gulf War, 27, 77
Pikayev, Alexander, 109, 111
Pine Gap relay ground station, 45
Powell, Secretary of State, 76, 94, 103, 122
procurement funding, 36
program definition and risk reduction (PDRR), 68
public scoping hearings, 95
Putin, President, 8, 17, 18, 20, 38, 39, 86, 92, 105, 106, 107

R

radars, 7, 9, 10-12, 14, 15, 53, 54, 56, 57, 67, 69, 78, 82, 102, 109, 110
RAMOS, 21, 66, 71, 72
Reagan, President, 14, 75, 79
research and development (R&D), 4, 7, 8, 35, 37, 44, 45, 67, 68, 71, 75, 77, 79, 84, 103, 104
Robertson, Lord, 119
rogue nations, 6, 77, 82, 83, 86, 87, 91, 99, 109
rogue states, 2, 4, 5, 40
Rumsfeld, Secretary of Defense Donald, 15, 16, 18, 64, 72, 76, 77, 84, 94, 103
Russia, vii, 3-6, 8, 12, 14, 15, 17-20, 38, 39, 40, 41, 45, 60, 79, 82, 83, 86, 87, 89, 91-93, 96, 99-108, 110-126
Russian-American Observation Satellite, 21, 66

S

Satellite Sensor Technology, 67
SBL Integrated Flight Experiment, 49, 50
Schroeder, German Chancellor Gerhard, 40
Sea-Based Boost, 43, 50-52
Sea-Based Midcourse, 21, 43, 54, 55, 57-59
Senate Armed Services Committee (SAC), 10, 11, 14, 15, 16, 24, 34, 35, 51, 55, 70, 71, 77, 82, 84, 96
sensors program, 66
Sentinel system, 79
September 11, 2001 terrorist attacks, 25
Sergeyev, Igor, 105, 108-110, 117, 118
Sergeyev, Minister, 92, 105, 108, 109, 110

Shemya, Alaska, 12, 13
shipbuilding, 26
shorter-range nuclear delivery systems, 114
simultaneous short range ballistic missiles (SRBMs), 62
Sino-Japanese relations, 44
Sino-U.S. relations, 44
South Korea, 60
Soviet Union, 5, 9, 11, 15, 17, 18, 77, 79, 82, 101, 102, 105, 106, 114, 119
Space Based InfraRed System (SBIRS), 2, 21, 53, 66-70, 72
Space Based InfraRed System, 66
Space Sensor, 21
Space-Based Boost, 21, 49, 50, 71
space-based Defense Support Program, 53
Space-Based Infrared System-Low (SBIRS-Low), 21, 66-69
space-based intercept program, 50
space-based kinetic energy experiment (SBX), 49
space-based laser (SBL), 49-51
space-based sensors, 79, 81, 82, 91, 94, 103, 109
space-based weapons, 84
Spain, 40
spiral development, 31, 34, 67
SS-27 missiles, 38, 112, 113, 114
Standing Consultative Commission (SCC), 11-13, 102, 122
START I, 38, 111, 113
START II, 38, 92, 111, 112, 113
Stennis Space Flight Center, 49
Strategic Arms Reduction Treaties, 38
strategic arms reduction treaties, 87
Strategic Defense Initiative (SDI), 4, 27, 29, 41, 49, 79
strategic stability, 38, 83, 91, 92, 99, 101, 105-112, 121, 123, 126
strategic weapons balance, 40

successor states, 17, 18

T

Taiwan, 42, 60
technical feasibility, 89, 91, 124
technological challenges, 4
Tenet, George, 89
terminal layer, 29
terrorism groups, vii
terrorists, 1, 5
test bed, 12, 13, 37
test ranges, 10, 13
theater ballistic missiles (TAMS), 66
Theater High Altitude Area Defense (THAAD), 14, 21, 27, 59, 61, 62, 70, 72
theater missile defense (TMD), 1, 5, 6, 12, 14, 24, 25, 43, 62, 76, 80, 107, 111, 122
theater-range missiles, 43, 44
Treaty regime, 19, 122
Turkey, 64

U

U.S. allies, 4, 5, 39, 40, 93, 100, 113, 115, 125
U.S. deterrence theory, 1
U.S. missile defense plans, 38, 122, 124, 125
U.S. missile defense tests, 18, 39
U.S. territory, 1, 5, 7, 10, 89, 99, 100, 105, 108
Ukraine, 18, 102, 112
United Kingdom, 64

USSR, 9, 108

V

Vandenberg Air Force Base, 15
vertical launch system (VLS), 56, 57

W

Walpole, Robert, 88
warheads, 24, 27, 29, 30, 38, 42, 47, 54, 85, 87, 89, 90, 92, 100, 109, 111-113
weapons of mass destruction, vii, 1, 5, 24, 40, 41, 71, 86, 92, 107
Welch panel, 90
withdrawal, vii, 1, 2, 8, 16-19, 38, 39, 84, 92-94, 104, 112, 125
Wolfowitz, Deputy Secretary of Defense Paul, 8, 10, 15, 16, 103, 104
World Trade Center, 16
World War II, vii, 1

X

X-Band radar, 12, 53, 84

Y

Yakovlev, Vladimir, 112-114, 119
Yeltsin government, vii
Yeltsin, President, 92, 106